For Venice — may you stand strong & beautiful forever

Dear P,

There is not much I can tell you about Venice... you will have to come and see it for yourself. On the train coming here I could tell from the look in the people's eyes that they were proud, moved and longing... to be in Venice. Whether returning, or going for the first time, longing to be part of the Venetian dream, of the theatre that goes on night and day among Venetian pillars. The unsuspecting car traveller could hardly guess, upon nearing Venice, that below the tangled web of highway could lie such a pearl. The city is like a beautiful mysterious woman who everyone wants to watch and stand as close to as possible; an ever-changing powerful lady who flows with the cycle of nature and commands profound respect for her beauty and uniqueness. Like a mermaid sprung unruffled from the deepest waters, she moves and gives with the tides. She is, I find, most beautiful from a distance.

These are the things I ate in Venice. From nearby shores, or inland, further out in the Veneto. Wonderful surprises let me say: things that you would never expect from glancing at the menus of the many tourist-drained locali. Mixed fried and grilled splendours, scallops served in their marvellous shells with simple dressings of olive oil, lemon and parsley. Lovely fresh and small soles, piles and heaps of shiny shells, people eating beautiful cicchetti, glasses of prosecco and other magnificent wines with meatballs, or fried sardines, and a selection of risottos suitable for any of the Doges. Wonderful ink-black spaghetti, or wholewheat pasta with a sauce of anchovies melted with onions till they die gently. From the fields beyond are faraona, or boiled splendid mixed meats with quince mustard, and liver melted with onions, and gloriously regal-red radicchios. And, I have to say, there is much to confront here: live eels and crabs, snails, raw fish pulled fresh from the waters to be plunged in salt water and served at once, if not raw.

The seafood, in particular, I am told, is best boiled in acqua di mare, so there is no danger of over-salting or under-salting the water; it is always just right!

There are times, you know, when I feel I am a part of the water. Even tucked up in my room with a shawl around me, I can smell the water. I have spray on my boots still from earlier when I was coming home to keep dry. And I can hear the water outside, splashing up out of the canal, joining with the rain and dropping back like a duet, into the canal again. And on this we are all afloat.

Venice is like when you hear a piece of music that scoops down into your soul, or notice a real tear getting ready to drop from the eye of an unlucky child. One of those rare moments when you grasp the magnificence of this world. Yes, Venice is one of those moments.

You will have to come yourself and see,

Love, Tess

Xxx

EATING IN VENICE ⌇

_A meal could begin with a glass of Venice's lovely sparkling PROSECCO, and then continue with one of the very fine wines from the area such as soave or valpolicella.
CICCHETTI (or chicchetti) are unique to Venice; delicious bites served at any time (although normally appreciated before lunch or dinner). They are often on display as a snack that could end up becoming the whole meal. Sometimes served with a few toothpicks for picking up the bites with. There are special bars that serve only cicchetti.
In typical Italian fashion, most meals will begin with the ANTIPASTO, which might include a platter of the freshest seafood varieties, simply boiled and dressed and splashed with olive oil, lemon, parsley and some pepper. This bollito misto di mare is very typical and found in simple or rather more complex forms. It relies totally on the freshness and quality of the seafood.
Under the PRIMO category fall soup, gnocchi, pasta or rice, and these will be made according to the season or occasion. BIGOLI is the typically Venetian, slightly rougher, thicker, wholewheat spaghetti, which is wonderful, although various other types of pasta are served too.
RISOTTO is very much appreciated in Venice and can range from one or more of the many vegetables, fish or even meat. The type of rice used are carnaroli, vialone nano or arborio. To make a risotto the Venetian way: onda, shake, mantecare. Your risotto will need a broth to take it through its cooking process, usually just made simply with vegetables (brodo di verdure). Here is an example of a quick VEGETABLE BROTH:

Put 1.5 litres (6 cups) of water, 1 celery stalk, 1 small peeled white onion, 1 large peeled carrot, 1 thin-ish clump of parsley, any asparagus off-cuts, 10 or so peppercorns, 2 teaspoons of salt, 1 peeled and squashed garlic clove and 1 bay leaf into a large pan. Bring it all to boil, then lower the heat, cover and simmer for 20–30 minutes. Strain well, to make about 1.25 litres (5 cups).

__For SECONDI *you may find what is most on offer in the many restaurants and homes is the freshest of seafood either fried or simply grilled and drizzled with olive oil and some lemon on the side. This is a dish which relies, once again, on the incredible freshness and quality of the fish. And if you wade through the masses there are also many other Venetian dishes to be tried.*

__Many of the CONTORNI *or sides of seasonal vegetables come from the surrounding lagoon islands such as Sant' Erasmus, which supply many of the vegetables, in particular the wonderful artichokes that make their way to the markets and Venetian tables. The castraure, the typically small and lovely prizes, are the first artichokes to bud on the plant. Artichoke bottoms from the full-grown artichokes are much appreciated, too, and are often sold ready cleaned from buckets of water at the markets.*

__DOLCI *are many and varied to end the meal, or you might just have a few of the biscuits typical of the region with a glass of recioto, fragolino or grappa.*

Caffè. That's it. The Italian way.

Buon Appetito

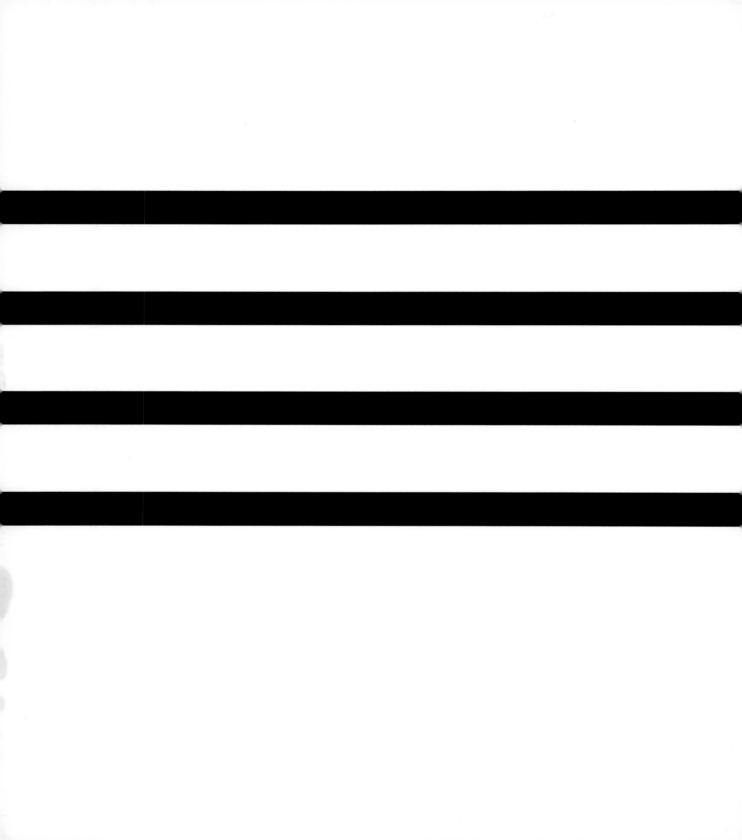

rules & rossini

Venice in its labyrinth & enigma; everywhere visible from the windows & mirrors on the top floor at Harry's Bar. Nothing tallies up. Even on Torcello at Locanda Cipriani there was a sudden dip in the grass that didn't seem as if it needed to be there. And the backdrop from the terrace looked like they had been told to recite & play & then the director had forgotten to call stop. Bridges; keyholes peeping into ancient courtyards full of secrets. Alleyways leading directly to steps that would take you right down into the canal if you let them.

I

ESSENTIAL RECIPES

Polenta *(fast & slow)*
Bread bangles Bussolai
Quince mustard Mostarda di frutta
Spritz
Bellini
Rossini
Pomegranate

Polenta

The Venetians are very attached to their polenta — they all know exactly how they like theirs & many people have a specific idea of when it should be served grilled or served soft. They are lucky to be able to buy the lovely white polenta, which is not easy to find elsewhere. This white polenta is cooked slowly until soft & is served under or next to so many dishes. As well as differences in colour (you are probably more familiar with yellow polenta than white), it varies in grain size. Coarse grained polenta, bramata, takes about 40 minutes to cook. Then there is instant polenta (lampo), which has been parboiled & cooks in just a few minutes.

When making soft polenta, the aim is to make it loose rather than stiff. The recipe here is a basic one that is soft enough to spoon well but not so soft that it won't support the accompanying sauce. You may have to test the amount of water you need for the type of polenta you are using to achieve the result that suits you best (use the package instructions as a guide). But if you are making it to be grilled, then make it a bit less watery than normal. In any case, judge the finished consistency, adding a little more hot water towards the end if necessary.

The recipe opposite is fairly plain & not very salty or buttery. It's suitable for serving with a saucy, flavoursome dish, or for grilling. If you would prefer, you can cook it in broth rather than water, or add a good blob of butter &/or a generous heap of grated parmesan. Another option is to either stir or tuck a few slices of cheese, such as taleggio or gorgonzola, into the polenta so they melt.

Luisa, my sister-in-law, has a great way to cook polenta without stirring it. You rinse a clean tea towel, wring it out, then cover the pan with the towel. Add the lid & make sure the ends of the towel are away from the flame. Simmer on the lowest possible heat for 40 minutes or so. Check it a couple of times but it should be OK.

If you're not serving the polenta at once, or you have leftovers (half the portion is a good amount for four), there are some lovely things you can make. One option is to pour the polenta into a baking tray to a depth of about 2 cm (¾ inch), spreading it with a spatula. When completely cool, cut it into wedges. Heat a chargrill pan or small rack on a barbecue. When hot, grill the polenta until solid ridges (not too black & burned though) form on the underside. Polenta cooked this way is often served with food in Venice, or it can be the crostino for a savoury topping, or even spread with a little jam for breakfast. To clean your polenta pot, simply leave it to soak in water for a while & then the polenta will peel away.

Fast

1 tablespoon olive oil
1 teaspoon salt
250 g (9 oz) instant polenta

This is the quick way to cook polenta, which in today's rush is probably the way that many make it.

__Fill a pot with about 1.5 litres (52 fl oz/6 cups) water, then add the oil & salt. Bring the water to the boil. Drizzle the polenta into the water, whisking constantly for a few minutes (or follow the packet directions) until it is thick & smooth. It should be a thick pouring consistency. If you think it looks too thick, add a little hot water towards the end. Serve at once.

Makes 8 cupfuls
Serves 4 as a main or 8 as a starter

Slow

1 tablespoon olive oil
1 teaspoon salt
250 g (9 oz) polenta bramata
  (or polenta flour) or white
  polenta (polenta bianca)

The long way:

__Fill a heavy-based pot with about 1.5 litres (52 fl oz/6 cups) water. When it is boiling, add the oil & salt, then the polenta in a thin stream until it has all been added, whisking in well. When it comes back up to the boil, lower the heat to as low as possible, partly cover with a lid & simmer for about 40 minutes, whisking often to make sure nothing is sticking & that it is smooth.

Makes 8 cupfuls
Serves 4 as a main or 8 as a starter

We are approaching San Marco on the Grand Canal & everything looks like paper cut outs. I preferred the smaller motoscafo that took me to Giudecca. I hate that on some vaporetti there is a hard metal line on the window that cuts everything in half at my exact eye level. I have to dance above & below the line to piece it all together. So typical & theatrical… like all of Venice.

Venice knows about aperitivo. How to do it well & even make a small occasion of it… like everything else. It is the place of the piazza or campo. Nice big squares, rectangles or any odd shape. For people to use as their gardens. A space to settle into for a while & watch Venetian vitality.

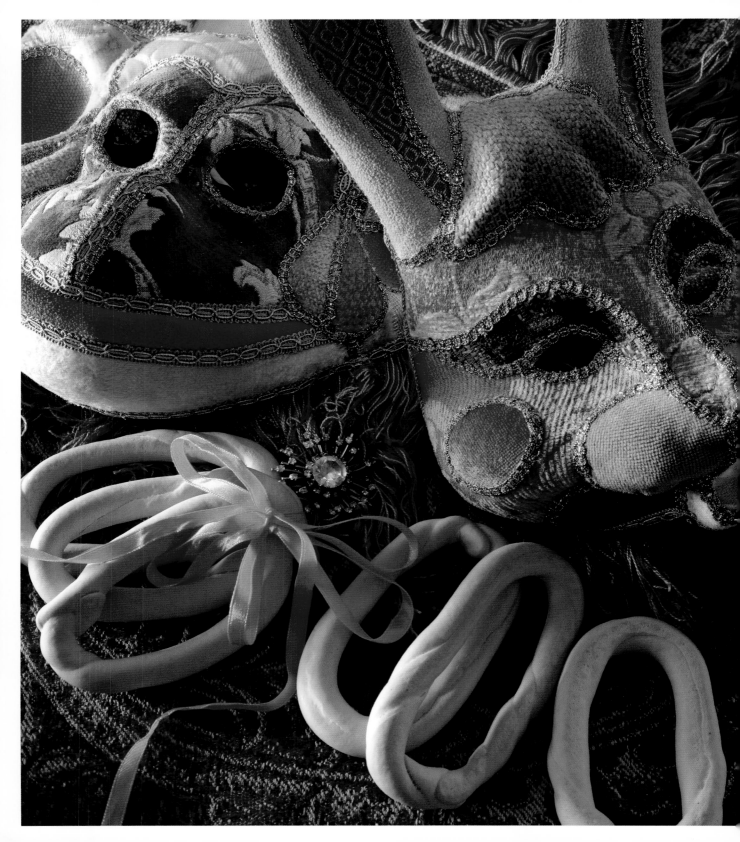

Bussolai

Bread bangles

15 g (½ oz) fresh yeast or
   1 tablespoon dried
1 teaspoon sugar
30 g (1 oz) margarine or butter,
   melted & cooled
about 500 g (1 lb 2 oz/4 cups)
   cake (00) flour
1 teaspoon salt

These are bread sticks in the shape of oval bangles — you'll find them served in the bread baskets all over Venice, much like grissini. You have to roll these thin or they will puff up like thin bread rolls in parts, although even if that happens it's no disaster. If you prefer, just roll the dough into rolls & bake — you'll get a wonderful plain, light white bread, much like the soft Venetian bread that, at first, I didn't like but do now. It's great for mopping up all the sauces at the bottom of your plate.

__Crumble the fresh (or sprinkle the dried) yeast into a bowl & add the sugar, margarine or butter, 100 g (3½ oz) of the flour & 250 ml (9 fl oz/ 1 cup) of lukewarm water & whisk together. Leave for about 10 minutes until the yeast starts to activate & bubble up a bit. Add the salt & all but 50 g (1¾ oz) of the flour (*you may not need to use it*).
__Mix it all together (*start with a wooden spoon & then use your hands*), adding a little extra flour to the dough & your hands if necessary, to get a nice soft ball. Knead for about 10 minutes until smooth & elastic. Make a cross on top of the ball of dough, put back into the bowl, then cover the bowl with a cloth & leave in a draught-free warm place for a couple of hours until it has puffed up well & doubled in size. Line 2 or 3 baking trays with baking paper.
__Preheat your oven to 200°C (400°F/Gas 6). Divide the dough into about 34 equal pieces or use your scales to measure each piece to 20 g (¾ oz). Using unfloured hands, roll each piece on a smooth surface to a thin rope 25–30 cm (10–12 inches) long, then press the ends together to make an oval 'bracelet'. Lift onto the baking trays.
__Bake for about 15 minutes until crisp & lightly browned. Best eaten fresh but you can store them in an airtight container or bag for 1–2 weeks.

Makes about 34

Mostarda di frutta

Quince mustard

350 g (12 oz) quinces
  (about 2 small)
1 litre (36 fl oz/4 cups) white
  wine
1 apple
1 pear
2 clementines or 1 mandarin,
  (about 120 g/4 oz total),
  peeled, seeded, segmented
  & skinned
50 g (1¾ oz) red & green
  candied cherries, halved
30 g (1 oz) mixed chopped
  candied citrus fruits
300 g (10 oz) sugar
a few drops of mustard essence
  or 1–2 tablespoons
  mustard powder

Luisa says at Christmas they eat Mostarda, mascarpone, & Baicoli. The beauty here is the few drops of mustard essence stirred into the cooled jam. Hopefully, you will manage to get some essence (which is not the same as oil & is difficult to get). If you do use essence, take great care as it is very potent — stand back & wear a mask if necessary to protect your eyes. Keep the essence in a hidden place in a cupboard far out of reach. We have given mustard powder as an alternative, which you should add to taste, but it's very much second best & tends to dull the colour. Another alternative is to serve the marmalade with a spoonful of mustard alongside.

__Wash the quinces & wipe away their fur. Quarter them carefully & tap away any falling seeds. Put into a pan with the wine, bring to the boil, cover & simmer for about 20 minutes until they are tender & can be peeled easily.
__Meanwhile, peel & core the apple & pear & chop up into rustic pieces.
__Remove the tender quinces to a bowl with a slotted spoon. Add the apple & pear to the wine, bring back to the boil & simmer, uncovered, for about 15 minutes until tender.
__Thinly peel, core & cut up the quinces, then return the flesh to the pan of apple & pear. Mix together, then lift out a huge slotted spoonful of the fruit. Purée the rest of the panful with a hand-held mixer. Add the unpuréed fruit back to the pan with the clementines or mandarin, candied fruit & sugar. Bring to the boil, stirring to dissolve the sugar, then lower the heat & simmer (*strongly at first*) for 1–1¼ hours. Mix now & then & halfway through turn the heat to very low & mix often so nothing sticks as it thickens & darkens. Once it's lovely & thick, leave to cool.
__Carefully add the mustard essence to the cool marmalade. Or stir in mustard powder mixed to a loose paste with a little white wine or water (*add it gradually until your preferred mustard flavour is reached*). Spoon into a sterilised jar & keep in the fridge for up to a month.

Makes about 750 ml (26 fl oz/3 cups)

Spritz

Red & orange

4–5 ice cubes

60 ml (2 fl oz/¼ cup) aperol or campari

60 ml (2 fl oz/¼ cup) white wine or prosecco

60 ml (2 fl oz/¼ cup) soda/ seltz

a thickish chunk of orange with skin

1 olive, shaken out of brine & threaded onto a cocktail stick

This is a much appreciated aperitivo in Venice. To make a Spritz, take a large wine glass & add a good splash of an aperitif, such as campari or its lower-alcohol version, aperol. Next comes a good splash of white wine or prosecco & a few ice cubes. A splash of soda water (club soda, or 'seltz' in the bars) is next because it revs everything up from bottom to top, & last, a piece of orange & a green olive on a cocktail stick. The olive is in brine & not rinsed, the lady says. The drink comes halfway to three-quarters up the glass. Very nice.

Everyone has their own way of Spritz. Use aperol or campari or whatever you prefer. Some people say no olive, others no orange, one wants a piece of lemon, one wants prosecco instead of the wine, one no wine at all — it's a bit how you take your coffee — rather personal. So here's a rough guide to how I like my Spritz. Adjust yours to suit your personal preferences.

___Put the ice into a large wine glass. Splash in the aperol & then the white wine, next a good whoosh of fizzy water to get everything moving & mixed in. Add the orange & olive on a cocktail stick. That's it.

Serves 1

❧ *Bellini* ❧

cin cin

1 beautiful sweet ripe white
    peach (about 150 g/5 oz)
a couple of raspberries
240 ml (8 fl oz) cold cold
    prosecco, or more if you like

Prosecco has its own kingdom in Venice. Not just any prosecco will do & there is even a separate wine list in some restaurants. Over many lunches I noticed people drinking full rounded plump bottles of chilled prosecco rather than wine, especially with their seafood… beautiful. Never mind stirring it into beautiful puréed white peaches & other fruits. These are the measures I like, but, of course, they're just rough estimates, depending on your glasses and such. They are easy to double or triple for more people, and add more prosecco or fruit, depending on your personal preferences. This is nice served with a raspberry, or you could purée a couple of raspberries and add, for a pinkier colour.

__Peel your peach with a sharp knife (or plunge it briefly into boiling water if the skin won't budge). Halve & stone the peach & purée until smooth. You can sieve your purée or leave it rough — either is good. You can add a little sugar & a drop of lemon if you like once you have tasted your purée (it will depend on your peach).

__Throw in one raspberry per glass. Pour the peach purée into large, beautiful, well-chilled glasses. Stir in the prosecco & wait for it to settle. Serve at once.

Makes 2

 Rossini

cheers

80 g (2¾ oz) ripe strawberries,
  rinsed
1 flat teaspoon sugar
  (or more depending on
  your strawberries)
1 teaspoon lemon juice
240 ml (8 fl oz) cold cold
  prosecco

*This is to be made when the strawberries are bursting with their best flavour.
I like to make it with small wild strawberries. The amount of sugar will depend on
your strawberries so taste & see.*

__Cut the green hats away from the strawberries & cut the strawberries into
pieces. Sprinkle with sugar & lemon juice. Purée until completely smooth.
Pour into 2 glasses. Divide the prosecco between the glasses, mix, wait for it
to settle & then serve at once.

Serves 2

 Pomegranate

alla salute

80 ml (2¾ fl oz) freshly pressed
  pomegranate juice
240 ml (8 fl oz) cold cold
  prosecco

*This is maybe my favourite for its gentleness of colour & taste. Use a citrus presser
here (or you could spoon out all the seeds into a wire strainer set over a bowl and
press them with a spoon to extract all the juice). A medium pomegranate will give
you about 80 ml.*

__Pour the pomegranate juice into 2 glasses. Pour the prosecco over. Serve.

Serves 2

prosecco & meatballs

I just went to La Vedova for prosecco. Stunning. He asked me three times to have a polpetta di carne. *So I didn't wait for the fourth (I should have listened to the first). It was a beauty. Big, like a golf ball. Minced beef with boiled potatoes — soft, soft, soft — fried in crumbs until red-ish gold & selling like hot cakes & there were other wonderful* cicchetti: *octopus, fried sardines, scampi,* baccala, *anchovies, boiled halves of eggs & delicious-sized glasses & carafes.* ⌐

II

CICCHETTI

Italian sandwiches	Tramezzini
Fried mozzarella toasts	Mozzarella in carrozza
Sardines sour	Sarde in saor
Scampi sour	Scampi in saor
Tiny baby octopus	Moscardini bolliti
Octopus & potatoes	Polpo con patate
Whipped baccala	Baccala mantecato
Meatballs	Polpette di carne
Fish balls	Polpette di tonno
Fried sardines	Sarde fritte
Roast sardines	Sarde in forno
Luisa's anchovies	Acciughe di Luisa
Andrea's anchovies	Acciughe di Andrea
Sergia's brew	Intruglio

Tramezzini

Italian sandwiches

The tramezzini are classic little sandwiches — white bread, stuffed to bursting with mayonnaise & other fillings — that have been updated by the cicchetti bars of modern Venice. They are an important part of Venetian life & are served often with a lovely glass of wine. You need squares of thin white bread with the crusts cut off (about 10 cm/4 inches square), which you then halve into two triangles. The tramezzini are stuffed in the middle & taper down on the corners. Keep them covered if you won't be serving them immediately, so the edges don't curl up. These are what we filled ours with:

__a layer of mayonnaise, then a small slice of ham & 2 artichoke quarters (*the ones bottled in oil*);

__a layer of mayonnaise, a tablespoon or so of crumbled drained tuna, 3 opened-out capers & a slice of hard-boiled egg in the middle;

__chopped/puréed blanched asparagus mixed with a little mayonnaise (*about 1 tablespoon mayonnaise to 1 tablespoon asparagus purée*), poached scampi, a couple of blanched asparagus tips & a sprinkling of ground pepper. Add a dab more mayonnaise to keep the top slice of bread in place;

__a layer of tuna salsa (from *Calamari con salsa tonnata* on page 212), some crumbled drained tuna, sliced pickled cucumbers & a dab more *salsa* on the top piece of bread;

__a layer of mayonnaise, sliced egg, artichoke quarters (*the ones bottled in oil*) & ground pepper;

__or any other filling you like.

Mozzarella in carrozza

Fried mozzarella toasts

Béchamel sauce:
1 scant tablespoon butter
3 teaspoons plain (all-purpose) flour
125 ml (4 fl oz/½ cup) warm milk
a grating of nutmeg

Dipping mixture:
2 eggs
1 tablespoon milk
a pinch of salt
flour, for coating
dry breadcrumbs

For 2 mozzarella & ham sandwiches:
4 slices pan carre or white sandwich bread, crusts removed
4–6 slices (not too thick) mozzarella
1 large slice of ham, halved or 2 small pieces ham
light olive oil, for frying

When in Venice it's great to be able to grab one of these delicious sandwiches for a snack. These are great at Rosticceria in campo San Bartolomeo — there they use tramezzini bread, which is very thin white crustless bread slices often in one long piece. When making these at home, you'll get a similar result with soft white sandwich bread. Use a small pan that will fit two sandwiches at a time so you don't need too much oil. The sandwiches are dipped in a batter before frying, but I found it simple enough to just dip them in beaten egg & then breadcrumbs for the crusty effect. If you like, whisk 3 tablespoons flour, ½ teaspoon baking powder & 2 more tablespoons milk into your dipping mixture, which is more how the Venetians would make this. Then you need not coat the sandwiches in flour first or in breadcrumbs before you fry. These are also good without the béchamel but then they are less creamy & soft inside. You can make the béchamel ahead of time if you like — it's fine to use cold.

___To make the béchamel, melt the butter in a small heavy-based saucepan. Whisk the flour into the butter & cook for a few minutes, stirring. Reduce the heat to low, then add half the warm milk, whisking well. Add the rest of the milk, a grating of nutmeg & some salt. Keep whisking until the sauce is smooth & thick, then remove the pan from the heat, cover & set aside to firm up a bit. Even completely cooled, this is fine to use.
___To make the dipping mixture, beat together the eggs, milk & salt in a flat bowl.
___For the mozzarella & ham sandwiches, spread 1 scant teaspoon of béchamel over all 4 slices of bread, right to the edge. Lay a piece of ham & 2 or 3 slices of mozzarella onto 2 pieces of the bread so that the topping comes right to the edge. Top with the other pieces of bread to make two sandwiches & press together firmly to seal well. Heat the oil in a pan — not too hot. Pat the sandwiches in flour, then dip in the dipping mixture to coat well. Shake them out of the mixture & let then drain off a bit, then press in the breadcrumbs to coat all over. Fry in the hot oil, turning when golden

For 2 mozzarella &
anchovy sandwiches:
4 slices pan carre or white
sandwich bread, crusts
removed
top-quality anchovy paste
4–6 slices (not too thick)
mozzarella cheese
2 large anchovy fillets in olive
oil, drained & broken up
light olive oil, for frying

& crisp on the bottom to cook the other side, then transfer to a plate lined with kitchen paper. Eat warm, taking care not to burn your mouth on the hot filling.

__For the mozzarella & anchovy sandwiches, spread 1 scant teaspoon of béchamel over all 4 slices of bread. Dab a little anchovy paste onto each piece here & there (*about ¼ teaspoon onto each*). Lay 2 or 3 slices of mozzarella onto 2 pieces of bread to come right to the edge, then top with pieces of anchovy fillet. Top with the other pieces of bread to make 2 sandwiches & press together firmly to seal well. Dip in the flour, egg & breadcrumbs & fry as above.

Makes 4

Sarde in saor

Sardines sour

about 125 ml (4 fl oz/½ cup)
olive oil
400 g (14 oz) white onions,
halved & thinly sliced
a few whole peppercorns,
gently squashed
2 bay leaves
125 ml (4 fl oz/½ cup) white
wine vinegar
15–18 whole sardines, about
500 g (1 lb 2 oz)
flour, for dusting
light olive oil, for frying

Every Venetian I have met loves sardines cooked like this — in saor means literally 'in a sour sauce'. My sister-in-law, Luisa, has fond memories of her grandmother often making a big glass bowlful. They make a great snack if you have a crowd to feed — not only because you can easily make many batches, but because they keep so well in the fridge. I think they taste best after at least a couple of days to soak up all the delicious flavours. If you are making a large quantity you may have to wash out the pan & start with a fresh batch of oil if the flour starts to burn. If you want to add extra flavour, do as many Venetians do & add a handful of pine nuts & raisins to the onions. I use smallish sardines — you can leave their tails on or off as you prefer.

__Heat the oil in a non-stick frying pan with a lid, add the onions & cook over medium heat. After a few minutes, add the peppercorns, bay leaves & some salt & pepper, put the lid on, lower the heat & simmer for 20–25 minutes. The onions must not brown but be well softened & nicely cooked, so check from time to time that not all the liquid has been absorbed. If the onions are browning too much, add a few drops of water & carry on simmering. Once the onions are soft & cooked down, add the vinegar & simmer without the lid for another 5–10 minutes until reduced a little, leaving the onions covered in a lovely sauce, but don't let them dry out.

__Meanwhile, to fillet the sardines, cut off the heads, then make a slit down the side of each fish & remove the guts. Open out the sardines like a book so they are still hinged together & place, skin-side up on a chopping board. Press each sardine lightly, yet firmly, to open out. Turn each over & pull out the backbone (*or leave in the bone & just clean them while you are eating them*). Rinse & pat dry. Pat well in the flour to coat on both sides.

__Pour enough oil into a large non-stick frying pan to cover the bottom abundantly. When the oil is hot add the sardines, turning them only when they are crisp on the bottom. If the flour is falling off the sardines & sticking to the bottom, you may need to reduce the heat a touch. When both sides are golden & quite crisp remove to a plate lined with kitchen paper to absorb the excess oil. Sprinkle with fine salt.

__Layer the sardines & onions in a compact bowl, seasoning as you go, creating about three layers. Add in the squashed peppercorns & a splash more oil if it looks as if it needs it. Cover & either leave at room temperature if you will be eating within the next few hours or put in the fridge where they will keep for a few days. Each time you eat a sardine, rotate the rest so that they are all covered & not just the underneath ones.

Scampi in saor

Scampi sour

18–20 scampi (langoustines,
  red-claw or large prawns)
125 ml (4 fl oz/½ cup) olive oil
400 g (14 oz) white onions,
  halved & thinly sliced
a few whole black peppercorns,
  squashed a bit
2 bay leaves
3 tablespoons white wine
125 ml (4 fl oz/½ cup) white
  wine vinegar
flour, for coating
light olive oil, for frying

*My friend, Sergia, once made me a whole wonderful batch of these to carry home
with me on the train & they were delicious. You could add 2 tablespoons of pine
nuts & raisins to the onion, or even use leek instead of onion. The scampi must be
lovely & fresh.*

__Peel the scampi. Remove the tail meat by cutting down the centre of the
underside of the tail with small sharp scissors & using your fingers to pull out
the meat. Devein, wash, pat dry & leave in the fridge.

__Heat the oil in a non-stick frying pan with a lid & cook the onions for a
few minutes before adding the peppercorns, bay leaves & some salt. Cover,
lower the heat & simmer for 20–25 minutes until well softened but not
browned. Check from time to time that not all the liquid has been absorbed.
Add the wine, let it bubble up a bit, then add the vinegar & simmer,
uncovered now, for another 5–10 minutes until it has reduced a bit & its
intensity has cooked out but it is still good & saucy rather than dry.

__Put some flour on a plate & coat the scampi well. Pour enough oil into a
large non-stick frying pan to cover the bottom abundantly. When the oil is
hot add the scampi, turning them only when they are crisp on the bottom. If
the flour is falling off the scampi & sticking to the bottom, you may need to
reduce the heat a touch. When both sides are golden & quite crisp remove to
a plate lined with kitchen paper to absorb the oil. Sprinkle with fine salt.

__Put half the onion in a small bowl, top with the scampi & cover with the
remaining onion. Scatter some pepper here & there. Add a splash more oil if
you think it needs it.

__Cover & either leave at room temperature if you will be eating within
the next few hours, or put in the fridge where they will keep for a few days,
soaking up the flavours more & more.

Moscardini bolliti

Tiny baby octopus

500 g (1 lb 2 oz) moscardini
  or baby octopus
1 small onion, peeled
2 garlic cloves, peeled
2 bay leaves
1 small celery stalk
1 small bunch parsley
about 8 peppercorns
2 tablespoons best extra virgin
  olive oil
juice of half a lemon
1 scant tablespoon chopped
  parsley
a pinch of peperoncino

This is nice as part of a mixed cicchetti plate. Use a great tasting extra virgin olive oil for the dressing — it will lift your dish to a different level. Moscardini are tiny red–purple baby octopus, weighing roughly 20 g (¾ oz) each. The Venetians also know them as folpeti. They are so small (only a bite or two) that they are often served with toothpicks & are just popped whole into the mouth. If you use the larger baby octopus, they can be halved or cut up into suitable sized pieces.

__To clean the octopus, cut between the head & tentacles, just below the eyes. Grasp the body & push the beak up & out through the centre of the tentacles with your finger. Cut the eyes from the head. To clean the head, carefully slit through one side, avoiding the ink sac, & scrape out any gut. Rinse under running water to remove any grit, then drain.

__Fill a pot with about 1.5 litres (52 fl oz/6 cups) of water & add the onion, a garlic clove, the bay leaves, celery, bunch of parsley & peppercorns. Season with salt, then bring to the boil. Add the moscardini, then bring back to the boil. Lower the heat, partially cover with a lid & simmer for about 30 minutes until tender (you may need to cook the octopus for longer for it to become tender). Remove from the heat & leave to cool in the liquid for a while.

__Cut the remaining garlic clove in half & rub it around the inside of your serving bowl, then leave the garlic in the bowl.

__Using a slotted spoon, remove the moscardini from the broth & add to the serving bowl.

__Dress with the olive oil, lemon, chopped parsley, peperoncino & a little salt & black pepper. Taste a little & adjust the seasonings, adding more of anything you think it needs. Serve at room temperature or even cold.

Serves about 6–8

Polpo con patate

Octopus & potatoes

500 g (1 lb 2 oz) octopus
4 tablespoons olive oil
½ white onion, chopped
2 garlic cloves, chopped
a good pinch of peperoncino
125 ml (4 fl oz/½ cup) white
*   wine*
375 ml (13 fl oz/1½ cups)
*   vegetable broth (page 12)*
500 g (1 lb 2 oz) potatoes,
*   peeled & cut into chunks*
2 tablespoons chopped parsley

This is nice as part of a cicchetti plate or just as an antipasto. It's very easy to double the quantity to serve more people, & you can also completely cook the potatoes separately & then turn them through the cooked octopus.

__To clean the octopus, cut between the head & tentacles, just below the eyes. Grasp the body & push the beak up & out through the centre of the tentacles with your finger. Cut the eyes from the head. To clean the head, carefully slit through one side, avoiding the ink sac, & scrape out any gut. Rinse under running water to remove any grit, then drain. Leave the tentacles reasonably long & cut the flesh into bite-sized chunks.

__Heat the oil in a nice wide pan with a lid & sauté the onion until soft & beginning to turn golden here & there. Add the octopus, mix through, cover, & cook over high heat until almost all of the liquid has evaporated. Add the garlic & peperoncino, turning through with a wooden spoon. When it smells good, add the wine & cook over steady heat (*uncovered*) until there is very little of it left on the bottom of the pan.

__Pour in the broth & bring to the boil. Lower the heat & simmer for about 30 minutes — covered for the first 10 minutes, then uncovered — until the octopus is very tender.

__Meanwhile, parboil the potato chunks for 10 minutes in a pot of lightly salted boiling water until just cooked but still firm, then drain.

__Add the potatoes to the octopus at the end of its cooking time when there is just a bit of liquid left, then simmer for 5 minutes together (*the end result is quite dry*). Check for seasoning.

__Turn off the heat & leave it to sit for 10–15 minutes so the potatoes keep absorbing any remaining liquid. Scatter with the parsley. Serve warm or at room temperature with some salt & a grinding of black pepper.

Serves about 8

Baccala mantecato

Whipped baccala

1 large garlic clove, peeled
   & squashed
125 ml (4 fl oz/½ cup olive oil)
500–600 g (1 lb 4 oz) baccala
   (salt cod), soaked
some small bread slices
butter, for frying

I don't know if many Venetian housewives really do make this themselves anymore – I think there are a few commercial places that make it fantastically well & people go there to buy it. I have also seen it made with some warm milk beaten in which gives it a whiter colour, though it may not keep as well. This is normally served on a crostino of polenta. Here it's served with small fried bread crostini, but is even good just with bread.

Baccala mantecato is the plain version; to make Baccala cappuccina, add 2 garlic cloves that have been well chopped to a pulp. Use a hand-blender to mash the fish well, drizzling the oil in very gradually until it's absorbed. Season with black pepper & whizz until creamy, then fold in 2 tablespoons of chopped parsley. Serve on polenta crostini. You can even spice it up by adding some crushed peperoncino, lemon juice or lovely fresh thyme as you mix.

Before you use the salt cod you need to soak it to remove the excess salt. Rinse the cod fillet first, then put it into a large bowl with enough water to completely immerse it. Cover the bowl & refrigerate, changing the water 3–4 times a day. Ask your fishmonger how long you need to soak the cod (it's usually 2–3 days). If you're unsure, test the cod by breaking off a small fleck, rinsing & tasting it. The tail part is always a bit more salty. In some places you can buy ready-soaked salt cod, which is very reliable & convenient.

__Put the garlic clove into the oil to flavour it for a while. Drain the baccala, put it into a large saucepan & cover with water. Bring to the boil then simmer, skimming, for about 10 minutes. Remove from the heat & set aside to cool for a while with the lid on. Drain. When still warm, remove the skin & bones & break into flakes in a bowl.

__Remove the garlic clove from the oil, then gradually drizzle the oil into the bowl of baccala, mashing well & stirring with a wooden spoon until all the oil is absorbed. Either use a hand-blender or food processor to pulse the mixture — so some is just bashed from your time with the wooden spoon & some is creamed. It shouldn't need any salt because of the baccala, but add some pepper. That's it — plain & stiff with a consistency a bit like chicken in mayonnaise.

__To serve, sauté some bread slices in butter with a dash of salt & pepper. Top with a good spoonful of baccala, pepper & an extra drizzle of olive oil if you like.

Serves many

Polpette di carne
Meatballs

450 g (1 lb) floury potatoes,
  peeled & cut into chunks
1 garlic clove, peeled
250 g (9 oz) minced beef
1 tablespoon chopped parsley
2 tablespoons grated parmesan
1 small egg, lightly beaten
dry breadcrumbs
olive oil, for frying

I ate something like these at Alla Vedova, a cicchetteria in front of ca d'Oro vaporetto stop. They were just fantastic. I noticed everyone having them with a beautiful glass of prosecco or vino before dinner. If you then carry on, as I did, with all the other cicchetti & more wine you can call it a day & a night & not need dinner.

These meatballs can be cooked in a frying pan or deep-fryer. The benefit of the deep-fryer is that they will keep their shape better, but it doesn't really matter. If you like, you can make smaller ones. I like them large because they fit in a frying pan in one batch & aren't too hard to turn.

You can also make these with part-boiled, mashed or finely chopped beef & some minced pork, so if you have some leftover chopped boiled meats, use them. This recipe makes simple, plain polpette but you could always spice them up a bit with a hint of chilli or any other herb.

__Boil the potatoes in lightly salted water until just soft. Drain, then mash until fluffy. Crush the garlic on a board with a sprinkling of salt until it is mashed to a pulp, removing any green bits if necessary. Add the garlic to the potato & mash together while still warm, then add the mince & a little salt & mash again, first with a masher, then with a fork until there are no lumps.

__When the potato has cooled down a little, add the parsley, parmesan &
egg & mix well, tasting a smidgen for any salt or pepper or whatever else you
think would be good. Put in the fridge for an hour (*longer, if you prefer*) until
they firm up.

__Grab enormous heaped teaspoonfuls of the mix, rolling them firmly
between your palms so you have big balls of about 5 cm (2 inch) diameter.
Put the breadcrumbs on a plate. Pour enough oil into a large frying pan to
come about 2.5 cm (1 inch) up the side of the pan.

__While the oil is heating, roll the balls in the breadcrumbs so they are
totally covered. Gently put the balls into the hot oil. Fry them without
moving until the undersides have a beautifully golden crust, then turn them
over with tongs or a spoon, taking care not to pierce them. Fry until golden
& crisp, then drain on kitchen paper. Sprinkle with salt & serve when they
have cooled down a little (*they are also good at room temperature*).

Makes 12–14

Polpette di tonno

Fish balls

225 g (8 oz) floury potatoes,
  unpeeled
185 g (6 oz) tinned tuna in
  olive oil
1 garlic clove, very finely
  crushed
1 small egg, lightly beaten
2 tablespoons chopped parsley
a pinch of peperoncino
light olive oil, for frying
dry breadcrumbs
lemon, to serve, if you like

You can quickly make up even half a portion of these anytime. These also work very well with crab. These are made much smaller than the polpette di carne & are wonderful as a cicchetto with a good glass of wine.

__Boil the potatoes in lightly salted water until just soft. Drain & allow to cool a little. Peel, then mash well.

__Drain the tuna & add to the mashed potato along with the garlic, egg, parsley, peperoncino, some salt & a little pepper. Mix together well, cover & refrigerate to firm.

__Heat enough oil in a non-stick pan to comfortably cover the bottom. Roll the potato mixture into small balls (*I got 25*). Roll them in the breadcrumbs & add to the hot oil, gently turning around when crusty so all sides are nicely done. Remove to a plate lined with kitchen paper to absorb the excess oil. Sprinkle a little more salt over the top & squeeze on some lemon juice if you like.

Makes about 25

The children of Venice are the luckiest ones. The most free. No cars. No worried parents. The ideal place for MONOPATTINI. *I pass them walking and hopping to school, passing by the forni to get rolls or focaccia, meeting friends and darting over small bridges, between canals while their parents chatter.*

&*Sarde fritte*&

Fried sardines

12–15 small sardines
  (about 250 g/9 oz)
2 very heaped tablespoons
  chopped parsley
2 large garlic cloves, chopped
1 tablespoon grated parmesan
1 tablespoon olive oil, plus some
  for frying
1 egg
dry breadcrumbs
lemon juice, to serve

These are lovely any way they come: just fried alone or with a few drops of lemon juice; at room temperature or even cold. Serve these alone or as part of a larger spread of cicchetti.

__To fillet the sardines, cut off the heads, then make a slit down the side of each fish & remove the guts. Open out the sardines like a book so they are still hinged together & place, skin-side up on a chopping board. Press each sardine lightly, yet firmly, to open out. Turn each over & pull out the backbone. Rinse & pat dry.
__Mix together the parsley, garlic, parmesan, olive oil & some salt & pepper & stuff gently inside the sardines (*I found I had just enough for my 15 sardines, using about ½ teaspoon for each*).
__Whip the egg in a small bowl with a smidgen of salt. Put the breadcrumbs into another small bowl. One at a time, pass the sardines through the egg, holding the fish still & tilting the bowl so no filling falls out of the sardines. Let the excess drip off & pat the sardines in breadcrumbs.
__Heat enough oil to generously cover the bottom of a large non-stick frying pan (*where the sardines will hopefully fit in one layer*). Fry until firm, golden & crusty underneath, then turn gently & cook the other sides. Lift out onto a plate lined with kitchen paper. Sprinkle with salt, pepper if you like & some lemon juice.

Serves 4–6

Sarde in forno

Roast sardines

15–18 whole sardines
   (about 500 g/1 lb 2 oz)
5 tablespoons olive oil
1–2 bay leaves
4 tablespoons dry breadcrumbs
   or 5 tablespoons fresh
3 heaped tablespoons chopped
   parsley
1 teaspoon dried oregano
1 teaspoon finely grated lemon
   zest
60 ml (2 fl oz/¼ cup) white
   wine

Use small sardines for this recipe. You can add any other herbs or spices you like here. This dish is also lovely at room temperature, which makes it perfect to prepare in advance.

__Heat your oven to 200°C (400°F/Gas 6). To fillet the sardines, cut off the heads, then make a slit down the side of each fish & remove the guts. Open out each sardine like a book so it is still hinged together at the tail & place, skin-side up, on a chopping board. Press each sardine lightly, yet firmly, to open out. Turn each over & pull out the backbone. Cut off the tail.
__Choose an oven dish that will fit the sardines compactly in a single layer but don't put them in the dish yet. Drizzle 2 tablespoons of the oil into the dish & put the bay leaves on the bottom.
__In a small bowl, mix together the breadcrumbs, parsley, oregano & remaining oil & season with salt & pepper. Mix well. Pat the sardines in the crumbs on both sides firmly but gently to coat well. Lay the sardines in the oven dish. Scatter the lemon zest over the top, then pour in the wine & roast for about 20 minutes until the sardines are golden & crusty.

Serves 4–6

Acciughe di Luisa

Luisa's anchovies

1 small red onion, finely sliced
3 tablespoons red wine vinegar
200 g (7 oz) fresh anchovies
   (about 12–15)
about 4 tablespoons polenta
olive oil, for frying
1½ tablespoons chopped parsley

Dressing:
juice of half a lemon
3 tablespoons olive oil

The size of anchovies varies greatly & this is also lovely if you can get small sardines (the preparation is the same). These are pressed in polenta, fried & then dressed with an onion, olive oil & lemon dressing. You can easily make a larger quantity if you like… they keep well in the fridge for a day or so & even stay crisp on account of the polenta.

__Put the onion in a bowl. Cover with cold water & the vinegar, leave for an hour or so, then rinse, drain & pat dry.

__To fillet the anchovies, cut off the heads, then make a slit down the side of each fish & remove the guts & bones. Open out each anchovy flat, hinged like a book with the tail on. Rinse & pat dry very well with kitchen paper.

__Pat the anchovy fillets in the polenta while your oil is heating in a non-stick frying pan. Fry the anchovies in a single layer (*or in two batches, depending on the size of your pan*) until golden & crisp on both sides. Remove to a plate lined with kitchen paper.

__In a compact bowl, make a layer of anchovies with some onion & parsley. Make another layer of anchovies, onion & parsley on top.

__Mix the lemon juice & olive oil to make a dressing & drizzle over the top so that it falls between the fish. Season with salt & pepper. Serve straightaway or cover & leave to absorb the flavours. This will keep in the fridge for a day or so (*after which you could add a bit more dressing if you liked*).

Serves 4–6

Acciughe di Andrea

Andrea's anchovies

200 g (7 oz) fresh anchovies
  (about 12–15)
125 ml (4 fl oz/½ cup) red
  wine vinegar
1 very small red onion, halved
  & thinly sliced
1 teaspoon salt
1 teaspoon vinegar
3 tablespoons olive oil
½ teaspoon dried oregano
black pepper
pinch of peperoncino

Andrea is Lidia's son (Lidia's asparagus are on page 252). This has little in common with the salty taste of anchovies as we are used to them — these are marinated to softness & wonderful with bread. For a different version you can leave out the vinegar & add 3 tablespoons prosecco, the juice of 1½ lemons, some small capers & a tablespoon of chopped parsley to the finished dish. You could even use small small sardines instead of the anchovies. This is a good dish for leftovers, as the anchovies can stay in their marinade for a day… so you could eat half now, half tomorrow.

__To fillet the anchovies, cut off the heads, then make a slit down the side of each fish & remove the guts. Open out each anchovy flat, hinged like a book with the tail on. Rinse & pat dry very well with kitchen paper. Lay flat in a dish in a single layer, slightly overlapping is fine.

__Cover with the red wine vinegar (*you may need more, depending on the size of your dish, as all the anchovies need to be just covered*). Cover with plastic wrap & refrigerate for several hours or up to a day.

__Put the onion in a bowl with the salt, vinegar & enough cold water to cover. Leave for 1 hour then drain & pat the onion dry.

__Drain the anchovies in a colander to drip all the vinegar away. Lay flat on a plate with a bit of a lip. Splash with the olive oil & scatter the onions over the anchovies. Crush the oregano between your fingers & sprinkle over the anchovies with some black pepper, peperoncino & salt if you like.

__These can be eaten straightaway or kept to marinade longer. They are even good the next day.

Serves 4–6

Intruglio

Sergia's brew

150 g (5½ oz) drained
    kalamata olives in oil
100 g (3½ oz) drained pitted
    taggiasche olives in oil
80 g (2¾ oz) drained large
    green olives
80 g (2¾ oz) drained sun-
    dried tomatoes in oil, halved
    lengthways
100 g (3½ oz) caprini (smooth
    goat's cheese), broken
    into chunks
about 200 g (7 oz) buffalo
    mozzarella, cut into chunks
½ teaspoon dried oregano
a good pinch of coarse crushed
    dried peperoncino
about 250 ml (9 fl oz/1 cup)
    good olive oil

This is delicious as an appetiser but is also fantastic in summer with tuna, or served over pasta. Intruglio is actually a Tuscan word that means 'brew' or 'concoction'. Although this is not a Venetian recipe, I feel that it belongs in the book because Sergia, who is the heart & soul of Venice as far as I am concerned, makes it & sells it in her alimentari in the Calle dei Do Mori. Originally, there were 27 alimentari shops in Venice; now there is one: Sergia's. She's like a mix between a great grandmother owl & a film star. I first met her when I stopped in at her shop & asked where she would send me to eat lunch with locals. So she closed her shop & accompanied me to her friend, Marinella & at 4 pm we were still drinking Valpolicella & chatting. Now, whenever I stand in Sergia's shop I am amazed by the amount of social goings on: the milk guy who pops in to exchange chatter & news, a quick visit from one of Sergia's seven grandchildren or other relatives, or a conversation with the man who knows about all the foundations of Venice. Sergia keeps introducing everyone & at the same time carries on calmly helping customers in her gentle way. Next comes a guy whom Sergia announces might give me a good recipe for goose, & so time goes on. Sergia knows every bridge & every alley of Venice & loves her city. She shows me her favourite places to sit for an aperitivo & enjoy special views. What a wonderful soul — so incredibly kind & helpful.

__Mix everything together in a large bowl — don't worry about being gentle. Keep covered in the fridge. As the oil chills & solidifies, the mixture will meld into one mass so that you won't be able to work out what it is, but once you remove it from the fridge, the oil melts. Store in the fridge, covered with the oil, for up to a week.

__Serve with bread, holding back some of the oil as it may be heavy. This is also lovely with cooked penne.

Serves many

clams & carpaccio

Giudecca is a beauty. Calm & serene. Great big water views, & no streams & streams of people. It is beautiful to just sit & watch, sipping spritz. This trattoria is the place from which to watch Venice — or the terrace at Cips. To watch Venice, Venetians, tourists, groups, singles, boats, activity… Everything bobbing up & down & carrying on quite naturally on the water. They all have Venice in their veins. ⚬

III

ANTIPASTI

La saltata di vongole e cozze in bianco

Clams & mussels

400 g (14 oz) clams in shells
350 g (12 oz) black mussels
4 tablespoons olive oil
1 small bunch parsley, plus
  2 tablespoons chopped
3 garlic cloves, 1 halved &
  2 roughly sliced
no salt
a pinch of peperoncino, if
  you like
bread & lemon wedges,
  to serve

This is the kind of thing you'll find in many restaurants. It is a lovely generous antipasto that could become a primo if mixed with pasta (you would need about 150 g/5½ oz cooked spaghetti to serve 2 people). It is also great served with a heap of chips to make a perfect secondo. What I love here is that the garlic is in biggish pieces that you eat with the clams.

Vongole veraci (carpet shell clams) are good here, but any not-too-small clams will work well. Your clams will probably have been purged of sand already but check with the fishmonger, otherwise you'll need to soak them for a day in a colander standing in well-salted water, changing the water several times.

__If you've been soaking your clams, give them a good swirl in the water, rinse them, drain & leave in the colander. To clean the mussels, you need to 'de-beard' them by pulling away those fiddly bits of algae that stick out. Cut them off with scissors or a knife if you can't detach them, then scrub the shells well with a wire brush to dislodge evidence of the sea. At this stage you need to discard any mussels that are open & don't close when you give them a tap.

__Heat 1 tablespoon of the olive oil in a large frying pan with a lid. Add the bunch of parsley, a grinding of pepper & the clams & mussels. Put the lid on & steam over a happy heat until they all open. There may be a couple of clams that don't open — give them a second chance but discard any that refuse to open. Lift the clams & mussels into a bowl. Pour the cooking liquid into a cup, checking at the same time that there is no sand. If you discover any sand in the cooking liquid, strain it through a muslin-lined colander. Wipe the pan clean.

__Add the remaining olive oil, the sliced garlic & 1 tablespoon chopped parsley to the pan. When you can smell the garlic (taking care not to burn it), add 125 ml (4 fl oz/½ cup) of the cooking water. Increase the heat to high & reduce the sauce, mixing the ingredients together. Once you have a nice sauce that is not too watery & not too thick (if it reduces too much it may be too salty), return the clams & mussels to the pan. Add the rest of the parsley, a grind or two of white pepper &, if you like, a pinch of peperoncino. __Meanwhile, toast a couple of pieces of bread, then halve them lengthways. Rub with the halved garlic & drizzle with a tiny bit of olive oil. Tuck the bread around the edge of the bowl or pan. Squeeze the lemon over the clams before eating.

Serves 2

As many times as I went out was as many times as I got lost. But I was never lost. I was always somewhere in Venice.

La saltata di vongole alla marinara

Clams & tomato

Tomato sauce:
4 tablespoons olive oil
½ small onion, very finely chopped
375 g (13 oz/1½ cups) tomato passata
a good pinch of peperoncino
2 tablespoons cream

Clams:
3 tablespoons olive oil
2 garlic cloves, chopped
1 kg (2 lb 4 oz) vongole veraci in shells
125 ml (4 fl oz/½ cup) white wine

This is how my lovely sister-in-law, Luisa (half-Venetian, half-Tuscan), likes to make clams. She adds a dash of cream to the tomato sauce, which makes it beautifully sweet & mellow. These can be served with bread or are great tossed into pasta with a little of the pasta cooking water to loosen things up. Try penne, spaghetti or any pasta you like: you'll need about 280 g (10 oz). You can also add a handful of chopped herbs to the sauce if you like. I have used vongole veraci (carpet shell clams) here but any vongole are fine. Your clams will probably have been purged of sand already but check with the fishmonger, otherwise you'll need to soak them for a day in a colander standing in well-salted water, changing the water several times.

__To make the tomato sauce, heat the oil in a frying pan & cook the onion over low heat until it almost disappears & is very soft (*it should not be dark but should be very well cooked*). Add the passata, a grinding of salt & pepper & a good pinch of peperoncino. Simmer uncovered for 10–15 minutes until it all thickens into a lovely sauce. Add the cream & allow the sauce to bubble for a couple of minutes more. Take the pan off the heat.
__If you've been soaking your clams, give them a good swirl in the water, rinse them, drain & leave in the colander. Heat the oil with the garlic in a large frying pan (*that has a lid*). Once you start to smell the garlic, add the clams & wine. Turn the heat up to the maximum & put the lid on the pan. Let the clams all steam open. Discard any that refuse to open.
__Take the clams out of the pan. Check for sand by pressing on the bottom of the pan with the back of a spoon. If you think there might be sand, then strain the sauce through a colander lined with muslin.
__Add all the clam water to the tomato sauce & simmer for 5–10 minutes until the flavours have merged & the liquid reduced a little. You want there to be quite a lot of liquid but it shouldn't be too watery. Return the clams to the pan & heat through for a minute. Serve straight from the pan with bread.

Serves 4

Capesante al forno

Scallops

1 large garlic clove, finely
   chopped
2–3 tablespoons lemon juice
1½ tablespoons finely chopped
   parsley
2 tablespoons olive oil
6 scallops with coral, on the
   half shell
dry breadcrumbs
2 teaspoons butter

This makes abundant saucy topping for 6 scallops, or even more if yours are on the smaller side. It's easy enough to double the sauce recipe if you want to use more scallops. You can buy scallops already prepared on the half shell.

___Heat the oven to very hot 220°C (425°F/Gas 7). Mix the garlic, lemon, parsley & olive oil together & drizzle generously over the scallops. Scatter with breadcrumbs (*a three-finger pinch per scallop*) & salt & pepper & put a small blob of butter on top of each.
___Put the scallops on a baking tray or in an oven dish lined with foil (*just to save on cleaning*) & roast for about 10–15 minutes until tender & with crusty golden bubbling juice. Serve with bread.

Serves 2–3

Moscardini al pomodoro

Baby octopus in tomato

400 g (14 oz) small moscardini
   or baby octopus (about 24)
4 tablespoons olive oil
1 tablespoon butter
2 garlic cloves, chopped
125 ml (4 fl oz/½ cup) red
   wine
500 g (1 lb 2 oz) chopped
   tinned tomatoes, squashed or
   briefly pulsed in the blender
1 bay leaf
1 or 2 whole cloves
a pinch of peperoncino
1 scant tablespoon chopped
   parsley
½ quantity soft polenta
   (page 21)

These exquisite little purple–red octopi are known as moscardini… their slightly larger cousins the Venetians call folpetti. This is also delicious as a sauce for pasta — in that case you should cut the octopus into pieces.

I ate this in a restaurant along with five other fish bits, followed by a fish lasagne, then a fritto misto & finally a crema di mascarpone with baicoli. I won't say that I felt fantastic as we waddled to the vaporetto to get home — but it was all delicious & rests now in my mind as a lovely memory. The children playing hide & seek through the tiny back canals while the parents were free. In such places, away from the thousands of tourists, the Venetians dine relaxed.

__To clean the octopus, cut between the head & tentacles. Grasp the body & push the beak up & out through the centre of the tentacles with your finger. Leave the tentacles whole if they're small, or cut in half if large. The heads can be left whole or halved if large.
__Heat the oil & butter in a wide (*not too big & not too high*) pan, then sauté the garlic for 1 minute until it smells good. Add the octopus. When much of the liquid is reduced & the octopus has a good colour, add the wine & allow it to bubble until slightly reduced. Add the tomato, bay leaf, cloves, peperoncino, parsley, salt & pepper & simmer, covered, for about 30 minutes, checking that nothing is sticking. Pour in ½ cupful of water & simmer for 15 minutes before adding another ½ cupful of water. Simmer for another 15 minutes, or until the tomatoes have melted down & you have a saucy, soft dish (*if necessary, keep cooking until the octopus is completely tender*). Taste for seasoning. Remove the bay leaf & cloves (*hopefully you can find them*).
__When the octopus is almost ready, cook your polenta (*or, if you're making slow polenta, allow the 40 minutes or so that it needs*). Serve a mound of the soft polenta in a bowl with a few of the pieces of octopus in the middle & some of the sauce over the top.

Serves 4

~Schie con polenta~

Mini prawns

about 250 g (9 oz) tiny prawns
1 bay leaf
3 tablespoons olive oil
2 teaspoons lemon juice, or more
   to taste
1 garlic clove, peeled &
   squashed a bit
1 scant tablespoon chopped
   parsley
¼ quantity soft polenta
   (page 21)

These prawns are often served as an antipasto or part of a mixed seafood antipasto in a smaller portion. Schie are miniature prawns & they are really, really tiny. It will seem crazy as you are peeling them. If you can't get schie, then use the smallest prawns you can find. Here they are boiled, peeled, then marinated in garlic & olive oil & served over polenta. Simple & good. You can add any other fresh chopped herbs or seasonings, but this is how I ate them in Venice. Lemon isn't often added to this dish but I enjoy the flavour. If raw garlic doesn't bother you, chop some of that in as well.

__Rinse & drain the prawns. Bring a small pot of water to boil, season it with salt, add the bay leaf & prawns. Bring back to the boil & boil for 3 minutes or so until it's all foamy on top.
__Drain the prawns, let them cool a little, then peel them & put in a bowl with the bay leaf, olive oil, lemon juice & whole garlic, plus pepper & extra salt if needed. Marinate for a couple of hours at room temperature. Sprinkle with parsley before serving over warm, soft polenta.

Serves 2

The Venetians, I sometimes found, were amazingly generous with giving directions but not always so amazing at sharing their recipes. They seemed to prefer directing, for the millionth time, a tourist to the fourteenth bridge, rather than be asked if they use white or black pepper with the clams. But I wanted the details of that garlic, hand-slivered by the grandmother...

Branzino marinato

Marinated bass

3 x 280 g (10 oz) whole
  branzino or other small,
  whole fish, filleted, skinned
  & boned
10 cm (4 inch) piece of tender
  celery stalk, sliced or chopped
about ¼ small red pepper
  (capsicum), cut into small
  thin slices
2 garlic cloves, peeled & a
  bit squashed
juice of 1 lemon
2 tablespoons olive oil
a pinch of peperoncino
1 tablespoon chopped parsley

This is lovely as part of a fish antipasto. You can serve this over some rucola, as I ate it in Venice, or just on its own. The fish isn't cooked over heat but the acid of the lemon juice will marinate it right through. It's important to have top-quality fresh fresh fish. Use white-fleshed boned fillets that are suitable for marinating, such as bass or bream (ask your fishmonger for advice). If you are using fish that has been filleted for you, you will need three 200 g (7 oz) fillets.

__First make sure that all the bones have been removed from the fish, then cut it into thin-ish rustic chunks & put in a non-metallic bowl. Add the celery, red pepper, garlic, lemon juice, olive oil, a pinch (*as large or small as you like*) of peperoncino & some salt & pepper. Gently mix everything together. Taste a little of the dressing & check that you are happy with it, adjusting the seasoning if necessary.
__Cover the bowl with plastic & refrigerate for 3–4 hours until you see that the fish is white & no longer translucent (this indicates that the flesh has been 'cooked' by the dressing). Gently turn the fish, taste a little & adjust the seasoning if you think necessary. Remove the whole garlic & sprinkle with parsley to serve.

Serves 4

Granseola in bella vista

Spider crab

500 g–1 kg (1 lb 2 oz–
  2 lb 4 oz) live crab (spider,
  mud, sand or similar)
1 celery stalk, roughly chopped
1 carrot, roughly chopped
1 onion, roughly chopped
a few peppercorns

Dressing:
4 tablespoons extra virgin
  olive oil
juice of 1 lemon
1 small garlic clove, squashed
1 tablespoon chopped parsley
a pinch of peperoncino

I couldn't get a spider crab at home when I needed it, so I got one in Venice & took it to a restaurant I knew & she gave me the cooking details. It is Marinella from La Buona Forchetta I have to thank. I then got another two from Alvise (from Osteria All' Antica Adelaide), who cooked them for me ready to bring home. Boiled, plucked, dressed plainly with olive oil, garlic, lemon juice — this is everywhere in Venice.

__Put the crab in the freezer for an hour or so to put it to sleep, & make sure you have some ice cubes ready for later on.

__Put the celery, carrot, onion & peppercorns in a large pot of well-salted water & bring to the boil. Add the crab, bring back to the boil, then cook at a rolling boil according to the crab's weight — less than 10 minutes for a 500 g crab (sand crabs) or about 15 minutes for 800 g–1 kg (mud crabs). Transfer the crab to a container of well-iced water & leave for 15 minutes to cool completely (*this will make the meat very tender*).

__Lift off the shell with the 'lever' on the underside. Clean off the guts & gills & gently clean off the muck, without immersing the crab or spraying it with water. Lift out the meat. Crack the claws with a sharp tap from the back of a knife to the back of the crab leg (*softer & easier to crack*) & remove the meat. Clean the shell & pile all the meat back into it for serving, putting the roe on top if your crab had any.

__Whisk together the dressing ingredients, season with salt & pepper & drizzle lightly over the crab meat.

Serves 2–4, depending on the size of the crab

BOVOLETTI

These are small snails to be boiled & dressed. The Venetian word for spiral is bovolo & these are everywhere, when in season. Bovoletti & polenta is a speciality for Redentore — the Saturday before the third Sunday of July has been a huge celebration since the 1500s, when Venice was saved from the plague. They build a floating bridge from the Zattere to Redentore Church for the weekend. Venetians take their boats with family & friends to Giudecca canal & spend the night, or part of it, eating & drinking wine. The snails are to be found at a fish store or market (even though they are not sea snails at all, but hill snails). Put them in fresh water which is to be changed three times (to purge the snails of their slime) & then heated up very slowly so that the warmth entices the snails to come out of their shells. Then zap them with a strong heat. Eat with garlic, olive oil, parsley & a squeeze of lemon if you like. Under the fireworks. ~

Carpaccio di pesce con pepe rosa

Fish carpaccio with pink peppercorns

1 garlic clove, peeled & halved

2 good teaspoons dried pink
   peppercorns

140 g (5 oz) thick tuna fillet,
   very very thinly sliced

140 g (5 oz) thick swordfish
   fillet, very very thinly sliced

3–4 tablespoons best extra
   virgin olive oil

juice of 2 small lemons

a pinch of peperoncino, if you
   like

1 scant tablespoon chopped
   parsley

leaves of 1 fresh thyme sprig

Venetians are used to pulling fish, such as cannolicchi (razor shell clams), out of the water & eating them very plainly there & then, but I have also seen many people enjoying plates of raw seafood, often dressed (as here) with oil & lemon. This is a bit of a variation with pink peppercorns. You can use any type of the freshest seafood such as scampi, cannolicchi, ciacale di mare (mantis prawns) & the like, or an oyster or two could be added. I have also made this with smoked swordfish, which was really good. There is no real need to marinate the fish at all — once the dressing has been added, it will be very tasty, but I normally marinate for anywhere between 10 minutes to 1 hour. One of the most important requirements is to slice the fish most finely. If you're not confident of your knife skills, ask your fishmonger to slice the fish about 2 mm (⅛ inch) thick.

__You will need two large plates with rims. Rub each plate with the garlic clove, covering as much of the plate as you can. Wrap the peppercorns in a thick piece of kitchen paper & gently press down with your palms to lightly crush them — it is nice if many remain whole, just lightly pressed to release their flavour.

__Lay the fish slices out flat, with the tuna on one plate & swordfish on other. If necessary, overlap the pieces. Dribble half the oil & lemon juice over each plate & scatter half the peppercorns onto each. Season with a pinch of peperoncino, if you like, & some salt & pepper. Leave at room temperature for 10 minutes or so. Once the fish starts to change colour slightly it's ready to serve. (*It could also stay in the fridge, covered, for an hour.*)

__Before serving, scatter parsley over one plate & thyme over the other (*I like parsley for the swordfish & thyme for the tuna*). Taste the fish & if necessary add a little more salt or other seasoning.

Serves 4

❧Carpaccio di carne❧

Meat carpaccio

1 beautiful artichoke suitable
  for eating raw
125 g (4 oz) very thinly
  sliced beef
juice of half a lemon
table & coarse pounded salt
2 tablespoons extra virgin
  olive oil
about 20 g (1 oz) shaved
  parmesan or asiago stagionato
bread, to serve

*Harry's Bar made this famous. The carpaccio there is excellent & is served with
a creamy mayonnaise sauce drizzled over. Here I have served it with artichoke &
a lemon oil. You could also serve it with rocket, or thin slices of endive, fennel or
celeriac. A couple of blobs of a creamy blue cheese here & there also work well. Serve
this as an antipasto for two or a secondo for one. It is lovely as a summer lunch with
a green salad on the side & some bread, & then it can take something slightly richer
for dessert.*

   *Use well trimmed & tender flavoursome lean beef such as girello or shell steak
(use strip loin or porterhouse), tenderloin (mid loin), or beef fillet works well. The
diameter of the meat is not important; just add more slices to the plate to cover it,
overlapping slightly if necessary. Ask the butcher to trim the meat for you. You may
even be able to convince him to slice it, but only if you plan to serve it within an
hour or two. If you slice the meat yourself, cut it very cold from the fridge to get the
thinnest possible slices. It is important the meat is thin thin & soft soft. Add some
coarse pounded salt in too for the texture — table salt with a small amount of bashed
coarse salt added.*

__Prepare your artichoke first. Trim away the outer leaves & cut a slice off
the top. Halve the artichoke & remove the hairy choke if it has one, then cut
each half into fine slices 1–2 mm thick. (*If you're not serving immediately, keep
them covered with cold water & a little lemon juice to prevent them turning black.*)
__If necessary, put the beef slices between two sheets of plastic wrap &
pound with a meat mallet until very thin. Arrange them flat on a large plate,
slightly overlapping is fine. Scatter the artichoke slices over the top. Drizzle
with lemon juice, sprinkle with the salt & drizzle with oil. Now scatter the
cheese on top & a good grind of black pepper. Serve with bread & perhaps
the bottle of olive oil, salt & black pepper on the side in case you need extra.

Serves 2

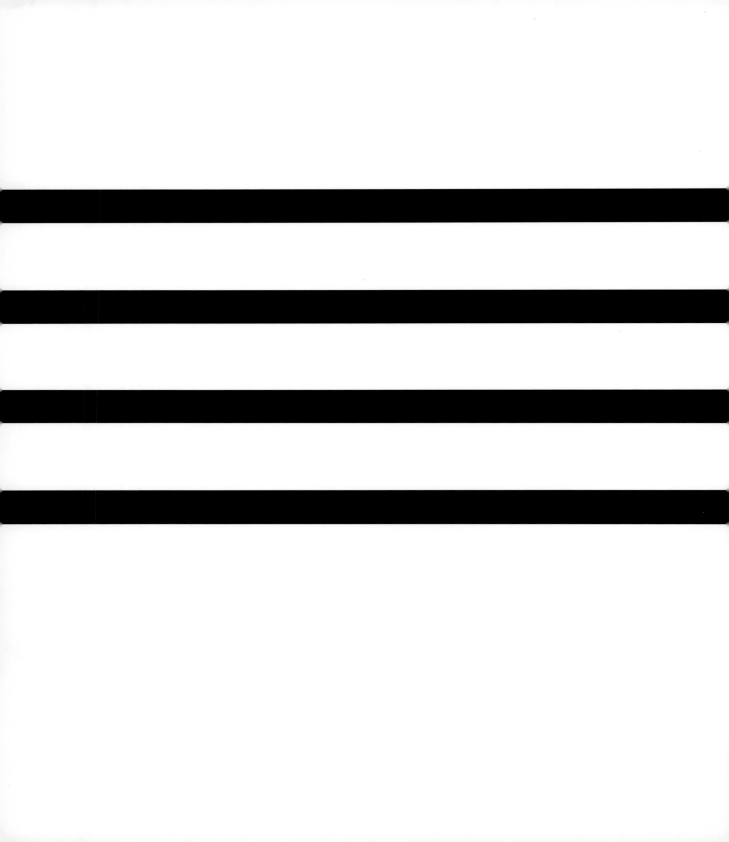

zuppa & zattere

The prize goes to who is out at the break of dawn. To watch the sun lighting up some pale colours & just start to brighten up the hyperbole. Follow the low crying of the seagulls. Early morning water & early-bird Venetians chatting, looking out for each other as they do. Witness the backstreet small events… Papà dropping his child off to school by vaporetto. I can see who reads which newspaper. I know the tastes of a gentleman's flowers after a few days & the colour of the old ladies' shopping trollies as they go to the market. One by one they all slip out of home & onto the stage set. ⚬

IV

ZUPPA / PASTA / GNOCCHI

Pasta & beans	Pasta e fagioli
Split pea soup	Zuppa di piselli spezzati
Fish soup	Zuppa di pesce
Healthy pasta with anchovies & onion	Bigoli in salsa
Scampi & gnocchi	Gnocchi con scampi
Pumpkin gnocchi	Gnocchi di zucca
Spaghetti with tiny artichokes & prawns	Spaghetti con castraure e gamberi
Crab linguini	Linguine al granchio
Spaghetti with clams & calamari	Spaghetti con vongole e calamari
Monkfish & bavette lasagne	Pasticcio di pesce
Seafood lasagne	Lasagne di pesce
Radicchio lasagne	Lasagne di radicchio
Spaghetti with tomato & scampi	Spaghetti alla busara
Spaghetti with fish	Spaghetti al ragù di pesce
Spaghetti with squid ink	Spaghetti al nero di seppie

Pasta e fagioli

Pasta & beans

300 g (10½ oz) dried Lamon
  or borlotti beans
1 carrot, peeled
1 celery stalk
2 garlic cloves, peeled but
  left whole
2 onions, peeled, 1 left whole
  & the other finely chopped
4 tablespoons olive oil
150 g (5½ oz) pancetta
  (unsmoked), chopped
a little pinch of peperoncino
1 tablespoon chopped rosemary
125 g (4½ oz) dry pasta, such
  as thin tagliatelle or tagliolini,
  broken up
thin slices of firm, mature asiago
  or pecorino, to serve
a drizzle of olive oil

This soup is served everywhere in Venice, made with various types of pasta. I particularly like this version that I ate at Marinella's restaurant, La Buona Forchetta, which she served with tagliolini that had been broken up & small triangles of mature asiago. When cooking it at home, you can use any type of short dry pasta (not fresh pasta). I've also seen it with torn & lightly dressed radicchio on top. You can make the soup beforehand & keep it in the fridge for a day (you will need to add water when reheating, though).

Lamon beans are the large creamy speckled beans found in the Veneto region. They need to be soaked overnight & then cooked for 30–45 minutes until tender. If you can't source Lamon beans use borlotti beans, which may need longer cooking & perhaps more water.

__Put the beans in a large bowl, cover with cold water & leave to soak for 8–10 hours or overnight. Drain & put the beans in a large pot with the carrot, celery, garlic, the whole onion & 2 litres (70 fl oz/8 cups) of water. Bring to the boil & skim the surface.

__Lower the heat, partly cover the pot & simmer from 30 minutes to 1 hour depending on the type & age of your beans & the heat of the stove. You want the beans to be soft & creamy but not too mushy. You may need to add 500 ml (17 fl oz/2 cups) of hot water midway through cooking so you have a good amount of liquid without it being too watery. Season towards the end of the cooking time with salt.

__While the beans are cooking, put the oil & chopped onion into a wider, flatter pot & sauté until the onion is softened. Add the pancetta & carry on sautéing until the onion & pancetta are golden but not too crisp. Add the peperoncino & some salt & pepper & stir in the rosemary for a minute or so on the heat then remove the pan from the heat & cover.

__Take the beans off the heat when cooked. Lift out & discard the whole carrot, celery & onion. Lift out an abundant slotted spoonful of the whole beans & put into the pancetta pot. Take 2 tablespoons of the chopped onion

& pancetta mixture & put into the bean pot — a fair swap.

__Purée the bean mixture in a blender until completely smooth, then return to the pot, add the pancetta & onion, stir briefly & bring to the boil. Stir in the pasta pieces & cook for a few minutes until tender. If the soup is too thick for your liking, add more hot water.

__Taste to see if you need more salt & pepper. Ladle the soup into bowls & top each bowl with a couple of thin triangles of cheese so they melt a bit. Add a drizzle of oil & a grinding of pepper.

Serves 4–5

Zuppa di piselli spezzati

Split pea soup

500 g (1 lb 2 oz) dried
   split peas
2 tablespoons olive oil, plus some
   for the croutons
50 g (1¾ oz) unsmoked
   pancetta, chopped
1 tablespoon well chopped
   rosemary
1 white onion, peeled
1 celery stalk (not too big)
1 carrot, peeled but left whole
4 slices country bread with
   crusts, roughly cut into 5 cm
   (2 inch) pieces
grated parmesan

The split peas in Venice are green but you can use yellow, if you like. If you aren't going to serve the soup immediately, you'll need to add water when reheating it, then stir well because you'll find that it has almost set into a thick block.

__Soak the peas in a big bowl of cold water for an hour or two. Drain well.
__Heat the oil in a large saucepan & sauté the pancetta lightly until softened & pale golden, being careful not to let it become crispy. Add the rosemary to the pan & sauté for another minute. Add the drained peas, stir well & then add the whole onion, celery stalk & carrot plus about 1.5 litres (6 cups) of water. Bring to the boil, skimming occasionally, then lower the heat & simmer well for about 30 minutes until many of the peas have dissolved. Stir to help the peas break up, then keep simmering for another 10–15 minutes, stirring often so it doesn't stick, until the liquid has reduced to make a thick soup. If it's still too thin, keep cooking until it thickens. Season with salt & pepper (*or save the pepper for serving*).
__When the soup is almost cooked, remove the carrot, celery & onion with a slotted spoon (*these won't be served but you can eat them anyway, if you like*).
__Meanwhile, to make the croutons, scatter the bread on a baking tray, drizzle lightly with oil & bake for about 8 minutes in a 180°C (350°F/Gas 4) oven until crisp. Sprinkle with salt.
__Ladle the soup into bowls, then add a grinding of black pepper, a good scattering of parmesan & a small bowl of croutons on the side for each (*& a pinch of peperoncino if anyone likes*).

Serves 4–6

∿Zuppa di pesce∿
Fish soup

Brodo di pesce:
4–6 large prawns
3 cicale, cleaned & left whole
3–4 whole small fish, weighing
  a total of 800 g (1 lb 12 oz)
1 large carrot, peeled & halved
1 celery stalk with leaves,
  halved
1 white onion, peeled
1 large garlic clove, peeled
1 dried bay leaf
about 8 peppercorns
1 teaspoon salt
1 bunch parsley

Soup base:
4 tablespoons olive oil, plus
  2 extra
1 small white onion, finely
  chopped
1 small carrot, very thinly sliced
  slightly on the diagonal
2 garlic cloves, chopped
1 tablespoon chopped parsley,
  plus a little extra
125 ml (4 fl oz/½ cup) white
  wine

When making the broth for this soup, it's worth seeking out cicale — a mantis shrimp popular in Venice that is known to make a lovely broth. However, if you can't get cicale then use an extra couple of large prawns, leaving these ones whole to add their flavour to the broth. You can also freeze any leftover brodo & use later as the base for a lovely plain risotto.

Use small whole fish for the broth… I like to use different types for their flavour — scorfani (scorpion fish), gallinella (gurnard), pescatrice (anglerfish), or bream, mullet, or whiting depending on what your fishmonger has in. I haven't used their flesh here for the soup but you can if you like — or you could use it to make fish croquettes (Polpette di tonno, page 57).

__Begin by peeling & deveining the prawns. Keep the shells & heads for the brodo & put the meat in the fridge to use for the soup.

__Put all the brodo ingredients in a pot with the prawn shells & heads & 1.5 litres (52 fl oz/6 cups) of water & bring to a gentle boil. Lower the heat, then cover & simmer for about 30 minutes. Remove from the heat & leave covered until it cools a little. Strain through a fine sieve so you end up with a clear broth.

__To make the soup base, heat 4 tablespoons of the olive oil in a wide heavy-based pan & sauté the onion until it is pale golden & well cooked. Add the carrot, garlic & parsley & stir well until you can smell the garlic, then add the wine. Let the wine bubble away until it's evaporated, then add the tomato & season lightly with salt & pepper & peperoncino. Simmer uncovered for 10 minutes or so, crushing the tomato with a wooden spoon so there are no lumps.

__Strain 1 litre (35 fl oz/4 cups) of the fish brodo into the pot with the tomato & slowly increase the heat, stirring to meld all the ingredients. Once it has come to a simmer, cook for another 5 minutes or so to allow all the flavours to mingle.

250 g (9 oz/1 cup) roughly
puréed tinned or peeled
fresh tomatoes
a pinch of dried peperoncino

4 slices country bread with
crusts, roughly cut into
2–3 cm (1 inch) pieces
olive oil, for drizzling
2 x 150 g (5½ oz) firm white
fish fillets
a little flour
1 garlic clove, peeled
2 tablespoons cognac or brandy

__Meanwhile, to make the croutons, scatter the bread on a baking tray, drizzle lightly with a little oil & bake for about 8 minutes in a 180°C (350°F/ Gas 4) oven until crisp. Sprinkle lightly with salt.

__While the croutons are cooking, remove any skin or bones from the fish fillets, pat dry with kitchen paper & cut into 3 x 4 cm (1½ inch) pieces. Coat them very lightly in flour, flapping them against your free palm to get rid of any excess. Take your prawns from the fridge & cut each one into 3 or 4 pieces. Coat them lightly with flour.

__Heat the remaining 2 tablespoons of olive oil in a large non-stick frying pan (it should just cover the base) with whole garlic clove. Pan-fry the fish fillets quickly over high heat until crusty golden on the base, then turn over & add the prawns, cooking until they just brighten & turn opaque. Lightly season with salt, add the cognac & flame the pan, standing well back. Sprinkle lightly with a bit more parsley & a grind of pepper.

__Dish the fish into four hot deep bowls & cover with boiling hot broth. Serve at once with croutons on the side.

Serves 4

Bigoli in salsa

Healthy pasta with anchovies & onion

9 salt-packed anchovy fillets

8 tablespoons olive oil

2 large white onions, thinly sliced

60 ml (2 fl oz/¼ cup) white wine

black peppercorns, coarsely cracked with a hammer or rolling pin

1 scant tablespoon chopped parsley

240 g (8½ oz) bigoli or thick wholewheat spaghetti

This is everywhere & no wonder, since it is made from such simple but beautiful ingredients — the typical lovely thick wholewheat spaghetti, plump anchovies in salt, onions & freshly cracked black pepper. Traditionally this dish was served at room temperature. Ceramic dishes of this would be laid out on the tables of osterie ready for the customers.

You could try this using red onion, or adding a sprig or two of fresh thyme to the onions while they cook. Or throw in a few small olives... Parmesan may not normally be served, but I love it here. Use thick spaghetti if you don't have bigoli. Black pepper is a must here.

__Rinse the anchovy fillets in cold water, then debone & pat dry. Heat the oil in a large non-stick frying pan, add the onions & cover with a lid. Sauté over low heat for 20–30 minutes... as Sergia says, they must die slowly in the oil. When you see the onions start to colour, add the wine & let it simmer briefly, then add 3 tablespoons of water, cover again & cook until the onions are soft & most of the liquid has evaporated.

__Add the anchovies to the pan, breaking them up over the heat so they melt into the onion a little. Add the coarsely cracked pepper & parsley & remove the pan from the heat.

__Meanwhile, cook the pasta in boiling salted water, following the packet instructions. Drain, reserving a little of the cooking water. Add the pasta to the frying pan & toss, adding a little of the cooking water if necessary to meld it all together. Serve with more black pepper.

Serves 3

Gnocchi con scampi

Scampi & gnocchi

9–10 scampi (langoustines, red-
claw or large prawns) — you
need about 150 g (5½ oz)
scampi meat
1 tablespoon butter
1 tablespoon cognac or brandy
1 tablespoon cream
1 tablespoon chopped parsley

Tomato sauce:
600 g (1 lb 5 oz) tinned
peeled tomatoes
3 tablespoons olive oil
½ white onion, finely chopped
2 garlic cloves, chopped
60 ml (2½ fl oz/¼ cup) white
wine
a pinch of peperoncino

Gnocchi:
650 g (1 lb 7 oz) floury
potatoes, washed but unpeeled
about 150 g (5½ oz) plain (all-
purpose) flour, less if possible

This will serve 4–6, depending on what else you're serving at the table. I am making the assumption that you would prefer a small serving of something rich & that you'll probably be following with a Fritto misto (page 182) or mixed grill, you may have already had a crab salad as an antipasto & you'll want space for some mascarpone cream afterwards, or perhaps you'll just manage a Sgroppino (page 268). Maybe you'll be lunching outside on a terrace looking at miles & miles of water or lagoon. Who can tell?

In Italy we get potatoes that say on the bag they are perfect for gnocchi. If that doesn't happen where you live, try to choose floury potatoes of a uniform size so they will all cook to more or less the same softness at the same time.

__First, clean the scampi. Peel, remove the heads & devein. Cut up the flesh into 3 or 4 pieces. Rinse, pat dry & set aside.

__To make the tomato sauce, put the tomatoes in a blender or food processor & pulse until quite smooth. Heat the oil in a large frying pan & sauté the onion until it melts & is pale golden but well cooked. Add the garlic &, when you can smell it, add the wine & let it bubble up until it has evaporated & the onion is frying again. Then add the blended tomatoes, some salt & pepper & peperoncino & simmer over low heat for about 15 minutes or until you have a nice loose sauce, not too thick. Add the cream and bubble up for a moment. Keep warm while you make the gnocchi.

__To make the gnocchi, cook the potatoes in their skins in boiling salted water until soft. Remove & drain. Cool a little, then peel. Pass the warm potato through a potato ricer. Mix in as much of your flour as necessary to make a very soft dough — the less flour you have to use, the better & softer your gnocchi will be. Cut chunks of the mixture off & gently roll out logs about 2 cm (¾ inch) thick, without pressing down too hard. Cut into pieces about 2.5 cm (1 inch) long.

__Meanwhile, melt the butter in a small saucepan over the highest heat until it starts fizzing. Add the scampi pieces & cook until they are golden on the bottom, all the liquid has evaporated & the scampi are once again frying in the butter & there are some crusty bits here & there. Add a little salt & when the scampi are golden in places & the flesh is bright white & soft, add the cognac & flame the pan, standing back so you don't burn yourself. Add the scampi to the tomato sauce.

__ Bring a large pot of salted water to the boil. Add half the gnocchi to the boiling water & cook until they bob up to the surface, then lift out with a slotted spoon & add to the hot tomato sauce while you cook the second batch. Once the gnocchi have all been added to the tomato sauce, increase the heat to high & add about 4 tablespoons of the gnocchi cooking water to loosen things up a bit. Fold everything together.

__ Allow the sauce to bubble away & toss the pan by flicking your wrist to coat everything rather than stabbing at the gnocchi with a spoon to mix together. Serve up at once into flat bowls or plates with chopped parsley & a grinding of black pepper.

Serves 4 (abundantly) or 6 (scantily)

Gnocchi di zucca

Pumpkin gnocchi

1.1 kg (2 lb 7 oz) pumpkin
1 egg, lightly beaten
about ½ teaspoon salt
about 200 g (7 oz) plain
    (all-purpose) flour
oil, for dipping
125 g (4 oz) butter
2 or 3 sage sprigs
a good grating of nutmeg
lots of grated parmesan

I learnt to make these from my friend Julia. This pumpkin gnocchi is made without potato & is wonderfully soft & sweet. You will not be able to roll out the puréed vegetable as you would with potato gnocchi; instead use two spoons to form quenelles. The amount of flour is very approximate here and will depend entirely on how much liquid your pumpkin contains. The quality of the pumpkin is really important so choose a sweet, bright orange one. When cooking, you need to cook & dry out your pumpkin well at the start without crisping it too much.

__Preheat your oven to 180°C (350°F/Gas 4). Line a baking tray with foil. Peel the pumpkin & remove the seeds. Cut the flesh into largish slices. Roast the pumpkin on the tray for about 30 minutes until tender but not too browned (*or they will be difficult to purée*). Transfer to a plate & cool a little.
__Purée all the slightly warm pumpkin as smoothly as possible so it is evenly coloured & there are no chunks in the finished gnocchi. Scrape into a bowl, add the egg & salt & mix well. Add the flour, mixing it in well (*try to put in as little as possible*), until you have a mixture that holds its shape on a spoon.
__Bring a pot of salted water to the boil. Pour some oil into a cup. If you are not going to be serving your gnocchi at once, have a slightly oiled or buttered tray ready so they won't all stick together while they wait.
__Put the butter & sage in a small frying pan & heat until the butter turns golden & the sage becomes crisp, but be careful not to let it burn.
__When the water is boiling, lightly dip 2 teaspoons in the oil, then form quenelles by passing the pumpkin back & forth between the spoons. Gently lower the gnocchi into the water then lift out with a slotted spoon when they bob up to the top. Put them in the heated butter or on your oiled tray.
__Sauté the gnocchi in the hot butter for a moment or so. Spoon onto plates, dribbling the butter over & around. Serve immediately with nutmeg, parmesan & black pepper.

Serves 4

Spaghetti con castraure e gamberi

Spaghetti with tiny artichokes & prawns

6 large, sweet prawns
  (about 250 g/9 oz), peeled
  & deveined
6 castraure artichokes
juice of half a lemon
140 g (5 oz) spaghetti
3 tablespoons olive oil
2 garlic cloves, chopped
2 tablespoons chopped parsley
40 g (1½ oz) butter
a pinch of peperoncino
60 ml (2 fl oz/¼ cup) prosecco
  or white wine

Castraure are small artichokes — the tiny bitter beauties that come from the Venetian vegetable garden island of Sant' Erasmus. If you can't find castraure use a couple of ordinary, larger artichokes instead. This is my kind of primo & definitely what I would order if I saw it on a restaurant menu. I adore artichokes cooked in all possible ways. Use large, fresh, sweet, succulent prawns: I used three per serving as they were large, but you might decide to add more. You can leave them unpeeled for effect, but cut a slit to devein & make them easier to eat with hands at the table…

__Rinse the prawns & pat dry with kitchen paper. Prepare your artichokes: if you're using tiny castraure just cut them in half; for larger artichokes, trim away the outer leaves & cut a slice off the top. Halve the artichoke & remove the hairy choke if it has one, then cut each half into fine slices 3–4 mm thick. (*If you're not serving immediately, keep them covered with cold water & a little lemon juice to prevent them turning black.*)

__Meanwhile, bring a large pan of salted water to the boil & add the pasta.

__Heat the oil in a large frying pan & add half the garlic. When you start to smell it, add the artichokes (*drained if they have been in lemon water*). Season, add half the parsley & sauté for a few minutes. Cook over steady heat for about 5 minutes until just tender but still with a bit of crunch, then lift out to a side plate, scraping out all the sauce so the pan is dry.

__Add the butter to the pan. When it's fizzling, add the prawns & turn to the highest heat possible. Cook until they have a gold crust on the bottom then turn & sprinkle with salt, peperoncino, the rest of the parsley & some black pepper. When the prawns are opaque with a deep gold crust here & there, add the prosecco & bubble up fast to give some good sauce in the pan.

__Drain the pasta (*saving a little of the water*) & add to the prawn pan along with the artichokes. Add a little pasta water if necessary to bring it together. Toss through quickly & serve with a prawn or two on top & black pepper.

Serves 2

Linguine al granchio

Crab linguini

160 g (5½ oz) linguini
4 tablespoons olive oil
2 garlic cloves, crushed
100 g (3½ oz) ripe cherry
   tomatoes, cut into thirds
2 tablespoons chopped parsley
about 140 g (5 oz) fresh
   crab meat

This is how Giorgia from the Rialto fish market would make her pasta — it is the simplest of simple. If you're buying a fresh crab, you'll need one that weighs about 500 g (1 lb 2 oz) to give you this amount of meat. This is very often served with tagliolini in Venice, & you could add a dash of peperoncino if you liked. If you want to buy a live crab & cook it yourself, follow the method for Granseola in bella vista (page 93).

__Bring a large pot of water to the boil, add salt & cook the pasta according to the packet instructions. When the pasta is nearly ready, heat 3 tablespoons of the olive oil & the garlic in a large frying pan (it will hold your pasta, too, later). Add the tomato & half the parsley. Cook for a minute or so, then add the crab meat & cook for another minute or so with a pinch of salt.

__Drain the pasta, saving a little of the cooking water. Add the pasta to the frying pan & heat for a minute, adding a little of the cooking water if necessary to bring it all together.

__Turn off the heat & add the rest of parsley & olive oil. Serve at once with black pepper.

Serves 2

Spaghetti con vongole e calamari

Spaghetti with clams & calamari

350 g (12 oz) clams in shells
2 calamari
140 g (5 oz) spaghetti
4 tablespoons olive oil
2 garlic cloves, chopped
3 tablespoons chopped parsley
125 ml (4 fl oz/½ cup) white
    wine
a pinch of peperoncino

The important thing here is timing: the calamari has to be tender & you need the seafood cooking while you par-cook the spaghetti. Then they can be tossed together at the right moment & the spaghetti can finish off its cooking in the lovely thick seafood sauce. I like to use vongole veraci (carpet shell clams). Your clams will probably have been purged of sand already but check with the fishmonger, otherwise you'll need to soak them for a day in well-salted water, changing the water several times.

__If you've been soaking your clams, give them a swirl in the water, rinse them, drain & leave in the colander. To prepare the calamari, firmly pull the head & innards from the body & wash the body well. Cut off the head just below the eyes, leaving the tentacles in one piece if they're small. Discard the head, pull the transparent quill out of the body & rinse out the tube. Peel off the outer membrane & slice the tube into slices about 3 mm (⅛ inch) thick. Pat dry with kitchen paper (*you should have about 170 g/6 oz cleaned calamari*).
__Meanwhile, heat 2 tablespoons olive oil in a frying pan that has a lid. Add half the garlic &, when it smells good, add the clams, 1 tablespoon parsley and 3 tablespoons white wine. Cover & cook over high heat until the clams open. Discard any that refuse to open. Transfer the clams to a large bowl, removing the shells from half of them. Add all the clam water to the bowl (*if you have any suspicions there may be sand in the cooking water you can strain it through a muslin-lined colander*). Wipe out the pan with kitchen paper.
__Heat the remaining oil in the pan with the rest of garlic. Add the calamari, 1 tablespoon parsley, peperoncino & a dash of salt. Cook over high heat until the calamari changes colour. Add the rest of the wine & let it reduce a little. Remove from the heat and return the clams & juices to the calamari pan.
__Meanwhile, cook the spaghetti in boiling salted water until almost ready. Drain, add to the seafood pan & toss over high heat to thicken the clam sauce until it coats the spaghetti. Serve with olive oil, black pepper & parsley.

Serves 2

For all the water surrounding me in Venice, for all the time spent on it and watching it, there is relatively little swimming potential. I kept wishing I could dive in and I couldn't. There are so many places with much less water… and a lot more possibility for swimming.

Pasticcio di pesce

Monkfish & bavette lasagne

1.4 kg (3 lb 2 oz) whole
  monkfish, scaled & gutted or
  1 monkfish head, eyes
  & tongue removed
4 tablespoons olive oil
1 large onion, chopped
2 garlic cloves, chopped
125 ml (4 fl oz/½ cup) white
  wine
a good grating of nutmeg
2 sprigs of thyme
1 small peperoncino, crumbled
1 tablespoon chopped parsley
250 g (9 oz/1 cup) tomato
  passata
200 g (7 oz) bavette pasta
  (or other dry pasta)
3 tablespoons grated parmesan

Béchamel sauce:
100 g (3½ oz) butter
70 g (2½ oz) plain
  (all-purpose) flour
a good grating of nutmeg
750 ml (26 fl oz/3 cups)
  warm milk

This is Lidia from Lido's wonderful recipe for coda di rospo (monkfish). You must try it — it's a beauty & well worth the effort. You buy a whole fish & use the head to make this flavourful pasta 'pie' & the rest of it for a second course of mixed grilled fish (page 186) with salad or have the Monkfish with tomato (page 187) the next day. The recipe is designed for monkfish but you could use snapper, though I can't promise the flavour will be the same. If you prefer, use the tail instead of the head for this recipe: just cook the fish in the same way, then remove all the bones & mash the flesh into the ragù — you will get more meat, but it will also be less gelatinous than the head. If some of the steps sound too challenging, ask your fishmonger to prepare the fish for you, then you just have to take out all the bones with your fingers, using gloves if necessary, squashing the meat between your fingers as though playing with sand. All this removing of eyes & teeth might seem like a nightmare — but once you've tasted it you'll forget the details. The thyme is great here & oregano or marjoram would be just as good.

This meal is lovely the next day too: just cover with foil & reheat in the oven.

___If you are using the whole fish, skin it completely. Cut the head away from the body. Cut away the fins to make a neat tail with central bone. Set the tail end aside to use for stock or another dish.

___Heat 3 tablespoons of the oil in a wide pan that has a lid & sauté the onion until very soft, then add the garlic, cooking briefly before adding the fish head. Sauté the fish until well coloured on both sides, then pour in the wine. Allow the wine to bubble away until it has evaporated a little, then season with nutmeg, thyme, peperoncino, parsley, salt & pepper. Add the tomato passata & bring to the boil. Once it is boiling, add 500 ml (17 fl oz/2 cups) of hot water, then cover & simmer for an hour until everything is soft.

___Allow the mixture to cool. When the fish is cool enough to touch, lift out the head & then carefully remove all the meaty bits, squashing down the pulp patiently with your hands to ensure only flesh remains & all the bones & teeth have been removed.

__Return the fish flesh to the pot. Remove & discard the thyme sprigs. Return to the heat for another 15 minutes or so until the mixture thickens, stirring so nothing sticks to the base of the pan.

__Preheat your oven to 200°C (400°F/Gas 6). Cook the pasta in boiling salted water & drain 2–3 minutes before it is completely cooked. Transfer the pasta to a large bowl & mix in the remaining tablespoon of oil. Allow to cool.

__Meanwhile, make the béchamel sauce. Melt the butter in a heavy-based saucepan. Whisk the flour into the butter, then add a little salt & pepper & the nutmeg & cook for a few minutes, stirring. Reduce the heat to low then begin adding the warm milk. It will be immediately absorbed, so work quickly, whisking with one hand while slowly pouring the milk with the other. When the sauce is smooth & thick, remove the pan from the heat & leave to cool (*it should thicken even more*). Adjust the seasoning.

__Once the fish ragù has cooled down a bit, stir the cooked pasta into it along with one-third of the béchamel. Stir through gently so it's all mixed in. You'll need an oven dish that's about 23 x 35 cm (9 x 14 inches) & is 5 cm (2 inches) high (*I like my oval dish here*). Dollop a third of the béchamel over the base of your oven dish. Tip the pasta & fish over gently (*not flattening it, but just shaking so it settles*). Dollop the rest of the béchamel over the top to more or less cover the mixture, then scatter the parmesan evenly over the top. Bake for about 20 minutes until a lovely golden crust has formed here & there. Serve warm to hot. This is close to stunning…

Serves 8

Lasagne di pesce

Seafood lasagne

1 kg (2 lb 4 oz) small clams
500 g (1 lb 2 oz) mussels
4 tablespoons olive oil
12 lasagne sheets (pre-boil
    variety), about 18 x 9 cm
    (7 x 3½ inches)
2 or 3 garlic cloves, peeled but
    left whole
about 125 ml (4 fl oz/½ cup)
    white wine
about 2 tablespoons chopped
    parsley, plus a small bunch
a blob of butter
200 g (7 oz) fillet of san pietro
    (john dory), cernia (dusky
    grouper) or snapper, cut up
    into strips
5–6 peeled scampi (langoustines,
    red-claw or large prawns),
    cut into thirds
3 tablespoons grated parmesan

Béchamel sauce:
100 g (3½ oz) butter
70 g (2½ oz) flour
625 ml (21½ fl oz/2½ cups)
    warm milk
a good grating of nutmeg

For this I use a rectangular dish of 35 x 25 cm (14 x 10 inches) where 3 layers of pasta fit exactly. If you prefer something smaller or an oval dish, which is fine, you will either need less pasta or you'll have to cut it up & turn it to fit in the dish. Use any seafood you like here. Your clams will probably have been purged of sand already but check with the fishmonger, otherwise you'll need to soak them for several hours in a colander standing in well-salted water, changing the water several times.

__Have your lasagne dish ready. If you've been soaking your clams, give them a good swirl in the water, rinse them, drain & leave in the colander. To clean the mussels, you need to 'de-beard' them by pulling away those fiddly bits of algae that stick out. Cut them off with scissors or a knife if you can't detach them, then scrub the shells well with a wire brush to dislodge evidence of the sea. At this stage you need to discard any mussels that are open & don't close when you give them a tap.

__Bring a pot of water to the boil, salt it & add a tablespoon of the oil. Cook the pasta sheets for the time indicated on the box or until almost cooked (*it will all go in the oven & continue cooking*). Remove, refresh in cold water & lay out the sheets on a tray lined with clean tea towels, making a couple of layers as necessary to accommodate all the pasta sheets.

__Heat 2 tablespoons of the oil in a wide heavy-based saucepan or deep frying pan that has a lid. Add a clove of garlic &, when it smells good, add the mussels & clams with half the white wine, a grinding of black pepper & the thin bunch of parsley. Cover with the lid & cook over high heat until all the mussels & clams open. There may be a couple that don't open — give them a second chance but discard any that are stubborn. Lift the clams & mussels into a bowl & strain the cooking liquid into a cup, checking that there is no sand. If you discover any sand in the cooking liquid, strain it through a muslin-lined colander. Reserve 250 ml (9 fl oz/1 cup) of the cooking broth. When cool enough to touch, remove the mussels & clams from the shells. Chop the mussels but leave the clams whole unless very large.

__Heat the remaining tablespoon of oil & a blob of butter in a non-stick pan. Add the fish pieces & scampi & a clove or two of garlic. Sauté very briefly over high heat until crusty here & there & just cooked. Season with salt & pepper, then add the rest of the wine & reduce a little so it is still saucy. Remove from the heat & fish out the garlic. Add the mussels, clams & chopped parsley, tossing together.

__Make the béchamel sauce. Melt the butter in a heavy-based saucepan. Whisk the flour into the butter, then add a little salt & pepper & cook for a few minutes, stirring. Reduce the heat to low then begin adding the warm milk. It will be immediately absorbed, so work quickly, whisking with one hand while slowly pouring the milk with the other. Once the milk is finished, add the nutmeg & switch to using the reserved cooking broth. When the sauce is smooth & thick, remove from the heat & adjust the seasoning.

__Preheat your oven to 180°C (350°F/Gas 4). Assemble the lasagne. Start by dolloping 2 large serving spoonfuls of béchamel sauce into the base of the dish & cover with 3 sheets of pasta, overlapping slightly if necessary. The next 3 layers will be repeated 3 times: a good dollop or two of béchamel, one-third of the fish mixture & 3 sheets of pasta. Once you have added your final layer of pasta, spread 2 final dollops of béchamel abundantly over the top. Lightly tap the dish to let the lasagne settle. Sprinkle parmesan over the top then bake for 20–30 minutes until partly golden. Cool slightly before cutting. Serve with a thin drizzle of good olive oil on the plate.

Serves quite a few

Lasagne di radicchio

Radicchio lasagne

800 g (1 lb 12 oz) radicchio
  di Treviso
6 tablespoons olive oil
1 onion, thinly sliced
60 ml (2 fl oz/¼ cup) white
  wine
12 pasta sheets (pre-boil
  variety), about 18 x 9 cm
  (7 x 3½ inches)
6 tablespoons grated parmesan
a blob of butter

Béchamel sauce:
100 g (3½ oz) butter
70 g (2½ oz) flour
750 ml (26 fl oz/3 cups)
  warm milk
a good grating of nutmeg

This is as lovely & bitter as radicchio itself, so you have to like the beautiful leaf to appreciate this lasagne. The radicchio you will use here is the raddicho di Treviso, which is long rather than round. They vary in size, so you'll need between two & four for this weight. You'll need a rectangular oven dish that's about 35 x 24 cm (14 x 9½ inches) so the pasta sheets will fit perfectly — once they are boiled they swell up to larger than their uncooked size. You will need 9 lasagne sheets, but cook a couple extra just in case.

___Cut away & discard the tough white stalk from the bottom of the radicchio. Roughly cut up the rest into chunky strips along the length, wash & drain.

___Heat 5 tablespoons of the oil in a large frying pan & sauté the onion until soft & pale golden. Add the wine & cook until evaporated. Add the radicchio, cover & simmer over low heat until it surrenders its hardness. Add salt & pepper & cook, stirring now & then with a wooden spoon, until it is soft & there is hardly any liquid left in the pan. Remove the pan lid for the last 5 minutes or so.

___Bring a pot of water to the boil, then salt it & add the last tablespoon of oil. Cook the pasta sheets for the time indicated on the box or until almost cooked (*it will all go in the oven & continue cooking*). Remove, refresh in cold water & lay out the sheets on a tray lined with clean tea towels, making a couple of layers as necessary to accommodate all the pasta sheets.

___Make the béchamel sauce. Melt the butter in a heavy-based saucepan. Whisk the flour into the butter, then add a little salt & pepper & cook for a few minutes, stirring. Reduce the heat to low then begin adding the warm milk. It will be immediately absorbed, so work quickly, whisking with one hand while slowly pouring the milk with the other. When the sauce is smooth & thick, add the nutmeg, remove the pan from the heat & leave to cool (*it should thicken even more*). Adjust the seasoning.

__Preheat your oven to 180°C (350°F/Gas 4). Now assemble the lasagne. Dollop a couple of large serving spoonfuls of béchamel onto the bottom of the oven dish, spreading it to cover. Lay 3 pieces of pasta over the béchamel, overlapping them if necessary. Splatter half the radicchio (*not in a neat perfect layer*) over the pasta. Dollop some more béchamel over the radicchio & spread gently here & there. Scatter with about 2 tablespoons of the parmesan. Now add another layer of pasta, the rest of the radicchio, some more béchamel (*not all of it — save ½ cupful or so for the top*) & another couple of tablespoons of parmesan. Add the final layer of pasta & cover roughly with the rest of the béchamel. Sprinkle with the rest of the parmesan & add a few blobs of butter. Bake for 20–30 minutes until lovely & crusty here & there. Cool a little before serving.

Serves 6–8

Around the ghetto is something to see on a Friday night. It makes me sad not to be part of something so big. But they did invite me in for Kiddush & kittkah.

Spaghetti alla busara

Spaghetti with tomato & scampi

8 small–ish scampi
  (langoustines, red-claw or
  large prawns) with heads
  (about 6–7 cm/2½ inches)
3 tablespoons olive oil
½ small white onion, finely
  chopped
250 g (9 oz/1 cup) peeled
  tinned or chopped fresh
  tomatoes
a good pinch of peperoncino
1 tablespoon butter
1 bay leaf
2 garlic cloves, chopped
1 heaped tablespoon chopped
  parsley
60 ml (2 oz/¼ cup) prosecco
160 g (5½ oz) thick spaghetti

In the restaurants of Venice, the scampi are sometimes served whole with the shells & heads intact. It certainly looks impressive, but can be difficult to eat, so you decide whether you want to peel them. I recommend seeking out small-ish scampi & keeping the heads on for flavour but peel the bodies for easier eating. Some small scampi are quite easy to peel once they've been cooked, so they would be fine to serve with the shells intact.

__First, clean the scampi. Remove the shells from the bodies & devein (& *remove the heads if you prefer*), rinse & set aside.

__Heat 2 tablespoons oil in a pan & sauté the onion until completely softened, stirring often. Add the tomatoes, a pinch of peperoncino & some salt. Simmer, uncovered, for 10–15 minutes, squashing the tomatoes down with a wooden spoon occasionally, until the tomatoes melt & are free of lumps & you have a nice sauce. Keep warm.

__Heat the butter & the last tablespoon of olive oil in a large non-stick frying pan. When hot, add the scampi & bay leaf & sauté over very high heat until the base of the scampi becomes golden & forms a bit of a crust. Turn the scampi over, add a dash of salt, a pinch of peperoncino & then the garlic. Now add the parsley. Finish cooking the scampi until you can smell the garlic & both sides of the scampi are just cooked, then pour in the prosecco (*or white wine if you don't have prosecco*) & simmer rapidly until it has evaporated. The scampi meat must be soft but not overcooked.

___Meanwhile, cook the pasta in boiling salted water until tender. Drain, reserving a dash of the cooking water in case it may be needed to loosen the sauce. Add the spaghetti to the scampi pan & scrape the tomato into the pan as well. Toss everything together as gently as possible, preferably by flicking the pan to coat all & not mash things up. Add some of the reserved pasta cooking water if it seems too dry. Serve at once, with black pepper.

Serves 2

Spaghetti al ragù di pesce

Spaghetti with fish

120 g (4 oz) large prawns
    (about 6–7)
200 g (7 oz) clams in shells
200 g (7 oz) mussels
4 tablespoons olive oil
1 onion, finely chopped
2 garlic cloves, chopped
400 g (14 oz) tin chopped
    tomatoes (or fresh very ripe
    equivalent, peeled & chopped)
3–4 moscardini or baby octopus
    (85 g/3 oz), cleaned &
    chopped
a good pinch of peperoncino
5 cm (2 inch) piece cinnamon
    stick
2 whole cloves
125 ml (4 fl oz/½ cup) white
    wine
2 x 115 g (4 oz) boneless fish
    fillets, such as san pietro
    (john dory), cernia (or
    snapper), chopped
2 tablespoons chopped parsley
280 g (10 oz) spaghetti or
    bigoli

A 'ragù' like this might have been made by a fisherman's wife to use up the fish that was not sold that day. The fish would have been put into a terracotta pot with many spices & left to simmer slowly on the side of the stove. You can use 2 fillets of the same fish, or choose different ones. You could swap the lovely cinnamon & cloves here for some fresh thyme or other herb & a more everyday flavour. Use bigoli or a thicker spaghetti for this rather than a thinner one.

Your clams will probably have been purged of sand already but check with the fishmonger, otherwise you'll need to soak them for a day in a colander standing in well-salted water, changing the water several times.

__Peel & devein the prawns. Roughly chop the prawn meat & set aside. If you've been soaking your clams, give them a good swirl in the water, rinse them, drain & leave in the colander. To clean the mussels, you need to 'de-beard' them by pulling away those fiddly bits of algae that stick out. Cut them off with scissors or a knife if you can't detach them, then scrub the shells well with a wire brush to dislodge evidence of the sea. At this stage you need to discard any mussels that are open & don't close when tapped.

__Heat the oil in a wide pot. Sauté the onion until almost melted & pale golden. Add the garlic & once you start to smell the garlic, add the tomatoes, mashing them in with something like a potato masher. Bring the sauce to the boil. Add the moscardini, peperoncino, cinnamon & cloves & simmer, covered, for 40 minutes or so until the moscardini are tender. Check a couple of times that they are not drying out or sticking to the pan — if so, add more water. If necessary, cook for a further 10 minutes until they are very tender.

__Meanwhile, put the clams, mussels & wine into a pan, cover with a lid & cook over high heat. Let the clams & mussels all steam open. There may be a couple that don't open — give them a second chance but discard any that won't budge. Remove from the pan, reserving the cooking broth (*if you have any suspicions there may be sand in your broth, strain it through a muslin-lined colander*).

__Remove all the meat from the shells, discarding the shells. Chop the mussel & clam meat & add it to the pan with the octopus. Add the prawns, fish pieces, a tablespoon of the parsley & 185 ml (6 fl oz/¾ cup) of the clam & mussel broth. Simmer uncovered for about 10 minutes until it looks like a good ragù — rich & quite thick. Pick out the cinammon & cloves if you can find them.

__Meanwhile, cook the pasta in boiling salted water until tender. Drain well, reserving about ½ cupful of cooking water. Add the spaghetti to the ragu with as much of the water as you need to loosen the sauce, tossing through quickly & gently over the heat for a moment.

__Divide the ragù evenly among warm serving plates. Serve at once with a scattering of parsley & a grind of black pepper, plus a little extra ground peperoncino if you feel it needs it.

Serves 4

Spaghetti al nero di seppie

Spaghetti with squid ink

300 g (10½ oz) squid, with
  ink sac
3 tablespoons olive oil
2 garlic cloves, chopped
a pinch of ground peperoncino
1 tablespoon chopped parsley,
  plus some for serving
125 ml (4 fl oz/½ cup) white
  wine
140 g (5 oz) spaghetti

This is an aesthetically dramatic dish — jet black — which is how I like it, but if you prefer a softer look, add less squid ink. If your squid doesn't come with an ink sac or if it doesn't yield much ink, you can use a sachet of squid ink. These are sold by some fishmongers & delicatessens, often in a package containing 2 sachets of 4 g (⅛ oz) per packet. You should only need to use 1 sachet here, but you can add another one if you want the result to be blacker. Alternatively, you can make the sauce without any squid ink at all & mix it with black ready-made squid ink spaghetti.

__To prepare the squid, pull the head & innards from the body. Separate the ink sac from the rest of the innards without puncturing, then rinse gently & put in a bowl. Wash the body. Cut off the head just below the eyes, leaving the tentacles in one piece, & discard the head. Pull out the transparent quill, rinse the tube & peel off the outer membrane. Cut the squid body into 6 mm (¼ inch) strips & the tentacles into pieces. Pat dry with kitchen paper.
__Heat the oil in a non-stick frying pan that has a lid & add the squid. Cook over high heat until the liquid begins to evaporate, then add the garlic, peperoncino & parsley & season with salt & pepper. When you can smell the garlic, add the wine & bring it to a simmer. Once it is bubbling up, cover with the lid, lower the heat & simmer for 10–15 minutes until most of the liquid has been absorbed.
__Cut the ink sac into a cup & mix with 185 ml (6 fl oz/¾ cup) of water. Pour into the pan. Add a little more water to rinse out the inky cup, pouring it into the pan. Cover & simmer for 15 minutes or until the squid is tender (*check it's not drying out & add water if necessary*). Taste for salt.
__Meanwhile, cook the pasta in boiling salted water until tender. Drain, reserving ½ cupful of the cooking water. Add the pasta & cooking water to the pan with the squid & toss well to coat with sauce. Serve with a little extra parsley and a good grind of black pepper, even though you won't see it!

Serves 2

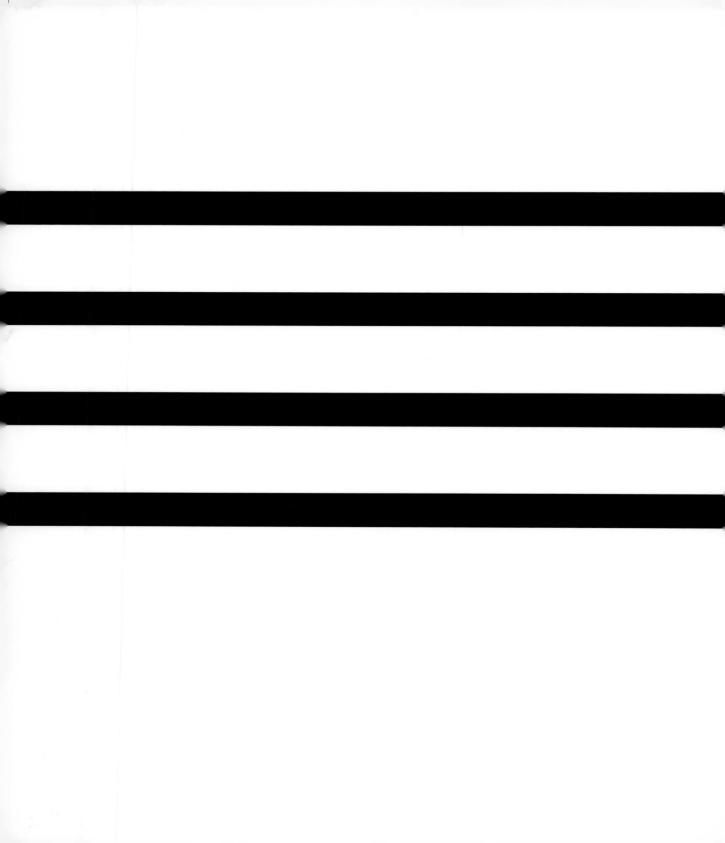

patience & risotto

There is a vaporetto etiquette to be followed. Move in quick. Don't loiter. Go straight inside or right to the other end to allow all the others to squash in too. (Unless you only have a couple of stops, then get on, sharp left or right near the opening — or proceed immediately to the other side if your stop will be on the other side of the zig zag.) Ideally, a sort of cross is left clear in the middle for passing through. Almost at your stop, you start pressing through the masses. Gently. Quietly. Without necessarily letting on that that is what you are actually doing. So that you happen to be on the side where you will be disembarking just before the vaporetto comes to a clanging kidney-jolting halt. If this hasn't worked, then you should say 'permesso' in a fairly firm kind of way to let people know that you urgently need to get past. ⊶

V

RISOTTO

Clam risotto	Risotto di vongole
Radicchio risotto	Risotto di radicchio
Seafood risotto	Risotto di pesce
Asparagus & scampi risotto	Risotto di asparagi e scampi
Vegetable risotto	Risotto di verdure
Rice & peas	Risi e bisi
Rice & potatoes	Riso e patate
Risotto with meat	Risotto con le seccole
Pumpkin risotto	Risotto di zucca
Milk risotto	Risotto al latte
Risotto with cabbage	Risotto con la verza

Risotto di vongole

Clam risotto

1 kg (2 lb 4 oz) small clams
  in shells
2 tablespoons olive oil
1 large garlic clove, chopped
1 tablespoon chopped parsley
125 ml (4 fl oz/½ cup) prosecco

Risotto:
2 tablespoons olive oil
1 tablespoon butter
1 small white onion, chopped
2 garlic cloves, chopped
4 tablespoons chopped parsley
280 g (10 oz) risotto rice
a pinch of peperoncino
60 ml (2 fl oz/¼ cup) prosecco
1 litre (35 fl oz/4 cups) hot
  vegetable broth (page 12)

I ate this in a restaurant where they used mussels & scampi as well as the clams, & their risotto had a ton of green parsley flecks that made me feel glad. The vegetable broth should have a delicate flavour – maybe add a spinach or chard leaf to the pot when you're making it. I loved using the prosecco, but you can easily replace it with white wine. If you like, add a few drops of lemon juice to serve. Rice is often estimated at 4 tablespoons per person as a starter portion in Italy.

I used lupini gandi clams, which are very good, but use whatever you can get. Your clams will probably have been purged of sand already but check with the fishmonger, otherwise you'll need to soak them for a few hours in a colander standing in well-salted water, changing the water several times.

__If you've been soaking your clams, give them a good swirl in the water, rinse them, drain & leave in the colander. Heat the oil with the garlic in a large frying pan with a lid. Once you start to smell the garlic, add the parsley, then the clams, prosecco & some white or black pepper. Turn the heat up to the maximum & put the lid on the pan. Let the clams all steam open – if there are a couple of clams that don't open, give them a second chance but discard any that refuse to open. Remove from the heat and cool a little.
__When the clams are cool enough to handle, take them out of the pan, reserving the cooking liquid (*there should be about 185 ml/6 fl oz/¾ cup*). Remove the clam meat from the shells – you can keep a few in their shells to garnish the risotto. Roughly chop them if they're large, otherwise leave them. If you think there might be sand in the cooking liquid, strain it through a muslin-lined colander.
__Heat the oil & butter in a wide heavy-based saucepan or a frying pan with high sides. Sauté the onion until golden. Add the garlic & 1 tablespoon of the parsley. Add the rice & peperoncino & stir well until the rice is coated with the buttery oil. You should not need to add salt because the clams are quite salty. Pour in the prosecco, lower the heat to a simmer & cook, stirring often, until almost all the liquid has evaporated. Add the clam broth & about

500 ml (17 fl oz/2 cups) of the vegetable broth & continue cooking, stirring regularly & adding another cupful of broth whenever it is absorbed, for about 20 minutes until the rice is tender.

__About 5 minutes before the risotto is ready, stir in the clams & remaining parsley & the rest of the broth if you think it needs it. Taste for seasoning. The risotto should still have some liquid & the rice grains should be slightly firm yet creamy. Serve with ground white or black pepper & a drizzle of great olive oil.

Serves 4

We stand up in the gondolas to cut straight across the canal. Just like Venetians. Legs apart so we don't lose our balance. We dare not sit down & seem like tourists — but learn to stand & balance.

*Once I get past the arriving and pushing through
the crowds, I sink into a glorious, soft and very
much present vitality. Past the muchness I find
simplicity. A marine serenity. Another reality.
A magical, acqua-coloured one.*

Risotto di radicchio

Radicchio risotto

about 500 g (1 lb 2 oz)
   radicchio di Treviso
4 tablespoons olive oil
½ white onion, chopped
about ½ teaspoon salt
250 ml (9 fl oz/1 cup) red
   wine
280 g (10 oz) risotto rice
1.25 litres (44 fl oz/5 cups) hot
   vegetable broth (page 12)
1 tablespoon butter
2 tablespoons grated parmesan

This is a lovely risotto with a beautiful rounded bitterness, not at all sharp. It's perfect for lunch on a winter's day or as a primo before a dish such as the Faraona (page 216). The radicchio you will use here is radicchio di Treviso, which is long rather than round. They vary in size, but about 2 large ones should give you this weight. For a different flavour, you could stir in 80 g (2¾ oz) grated taleggio or another cheese when you add the butter & parmesan at the end. Use a rice such as carnaroli or arborio. The Venetians like vialone nano for risotto because it absorbs large amounts of liquid & produces the wet, soupy style of dish they prefer.

__Cut away & discard the tough white stalk from the bottom of the radicchio. Wash well & drain. Cut into quarters lengthways, then chop along the length into rustic pieces.

__Heat the oil in a wide heavy-based saucepan or a frying pan with high sides. Sauté the onion until golden & well cooked through. Add the radicchio & salt & cook for 10–15 minutes until the radicchio collapses. Add the wine, let it bubble up & then add the rice. Bubble up for a few minutes to reduce the wine & mingle the flavours.

__Add 500 ml (17 fl oz/2 cups) of hot broth & continue cooking, stirring regularly & adding another 500 ml (17 fl oz/2 cups) more broth as it is absorbed, for about 20 minutes, or until the rice is tender. Just before the rice is cooked, add the rest of the broth (*you might only need half of it*) & mix to make sure nothing is sticking. The risotto should still have some liquid & the rice grains should be firm yet soft & creamy.

__Turn off the heat, season to taste & gently stir in the butter & parmesan with a wooden spoon. Serve at once with a good grinding of black pepper & lots of grated parmesan if you like.

Serves 4

Risotto di pesce

Seafood risotto

Brodo:

1 onion, peeled & cut in half

1 carrot, peeled

1 celery stalk

thin bunch of parsley

4 or 5 whole peppercorns

1 teaspoon salt

4 scampi (langoustines, red-claw or large prawns), unpeeled (about 200 g/7 oz)

4 prawns (about 150 g/5½ oz)

250 g (9 oz) small clams in shells

400 g (14 oz) mussels

200 g (7 oz) piece of firm white fish (such as snapper, mackerel, halibut or monkfish)

6 tablespoons olive oil

3 garlic cloves, 2 chopped & 1 left whole

3 tablespoons chopped parsley

250 ml (9 fl oz/1 cup) white wine

2 tablespoons cognac

250 g (9 oz) risotto rice

1 tablespoon butter

1 tablespoon grated parmesan

The Venetians have a wonderful selection of wines to drink & splash into their cooking. The sparkling white, prosecco, is much of a habit & will be often ordered throughout the meal.

I ate a fantastic version of this at the Trattoria alla Madonna, which is something of an institution — a huge space with 40 men in soft white jackets serving. Licio strode up to me like papa bear & made wise suggestions of what I should order (he should know: he's been there for more years than you'd guess). He took me right into the kitchen, threading me through the 40 waiters to see the 'onda' (wave), the shake, rock & roll that the chef does to 'mantecare' (mix & meld) the risotto at the end of its cooking process. Quite impressive.

Your clams will probably have been purged of sand already but check with the fishmonger, otherwise you'll need to soak them for a few hours in a colander standing in well-salted water, changing the water several times.

Peel & devein the scampi & prawns, keeping all the heads & shells. Cut the tails into 3 or 4 pieces & keep aside for now. To make the broth, rinse the shells & heads & put them in a pot with half the onion, the carrot, celery, parsley, peppercorns, salt & 1.25 litres (44 fl oz/5 cups) of water. Bring to the boil, lower the heat & simmer, covered, for about 20 minutes. Strain, discarding the solids, & set aside.

Meanwhile, if you've been soaking your clams, give them a good swirl in the water, rinse them, drain & leave in the colander. To clean the mussels, you need to 'de-beard' them by pulling away those fiddly bits of algae that stick out. Cut them off with scissors or a knife if you can't detach them, then scrub the shells well with a wire brush to dislodge evidence of the sea. At this stage you need to discard any mussels that are open & don't close when you give them a tap. Cut up the fish into pieces.

Heat 1 tablespoon of the oil in a frying pan with a lid, add the chopped garlic & sauté for a moment before adding the clams, mussels, 1 tablespoon chopped parsley & 125 ml (4 fl oz/½ cup) white wine. Cover with the lid &

cook over a happy heat until all the mussels & clams open. There may be a couple of clams & mussels that don't open — give them a second chance but discard any that refuse to open.

__Remove the pan from the heat &, when cool, pick out all the clams & mussels, reserving the cooking liquid. Remove the clams & mussels from their shells. If you have any suspicions there may be sand in the cooking water you can strain it through a muslin-lined colander.

__Heat 2 tablespoons of the olive oil in a small non-stick frying pan with the whole clove of garlic. Add the fish pieces, sauté over medium–high heat to just cook them, then add the scampi & sauté for another moment before adding a tablespoon of parsley, a small sprinkling of salt & pepper & the cognac. Flame the pan, standing well back as it lights up, & then turn off the heat & let it finish flaming. Keep aside for now, discarding the garlic clove.

__Now for the final risotto step. If necessary, warm the strained broth. Heat the remaining olive oil in a wide heavy-based saucepan or high-sided frying pan. Chop the remaining onion half & sauté until well softened. Add the rice & stir well for a minute or so until it is well mixed with the onion & coated with oil. Add the other 125 ml (4 fl oz/½ cup) wine & cook until almost evaporated. Then add the mussel/clam broth (*you should have a generous cupful*) & let it bubble away on a good simmer.

__When you see the rice puffing up & that there is not much liquid left, add about a cupful of the broth & cook, stirring, until almost all the liquid has evaporated. Continue in this way, adding more broth (*you'll need about 3 cupfuls in total*) & stirring for about 20 minutes until the rice is cooked. Season to taste. Once the risotto is creamy & cooked with some thick liquid, lower the heat & add the fish & seafood, butter, parmesan & remaining parsley. Now for the *onda...* This is the gentle shaking & rocking of the pan that melds the risotto together so that everything comes together like a sweet opera. Serve immediately.

Serves 4

Risotto di asparagi e scampi

Asparagus & scampi risotto

*12–16 scampi (red-claw,
    langoustines or large prawns)*

Brodo:
1 large carrot
½ onion
1 bay leaf
a few peppercorns

360 g (13 oz) asparagus
½ onion, finely chopped
4 tablespoons olive oil
250 g (9 oz) risotto rice
*125 ml (4 fl oz/½ cup) white
    wine*
1 tablespoon cognac
1 tablespoon butter
2 tablespoons grated parmesan

This is also good & delicate with just scampi or just asparagus. Some people don't serve parmesan with seafood, but I put a bit in here.

__To make the brodo, peel & clean the scampi & halve them down the middle. Set the meat aside for now, but rinse the heads & shells & put them in a pot with 1.5 litres (52 fl oz/6 cups) of water, the carrot, onion, bay leaf, peppercorns & some salt. Bring to the boil, then simmer for 30 minutes, then strain & keep the broth hot.

__Discard the woody ends from the asparagus & cut off the tips. Keep the tips on one side & chop the stems. Sauté the onion in 3 tablespoons of the olive oil until well softened, add the chopped asparagus & sauté briefly.

__Add the rice, turning it through so it is well coated with oil. Add the white wine & let it bubble up until much of it has evaporated. Add 500 ml (17 fl oz/2 cups) of broth, stir well & simmer for 10–15 minutes or until it has almost all been absorbed. Add another 2 cupfuls of broth, stir & cook for another 5–10 minutes. Add another ½ cup of broth if you need it for a creamy risotto.

__When your risotto is almost ready, heat the remaining oil in a small pan, add the scampi & asparagus tips & cook over high heat for 2 minutes, turning the scampi over when they have a pale golden crust underneath. Add the cognac, stand back & flame the pan. Add a bit of salt & toss it all together, then take off the heat.

__Stir the butter & parmesan into the risotto, then tip the scampi & asparagus tips into the risotto. Add salt if needed, quickly toss it all through & serve at once with black pepper.

Serves 4

Risotto di verdure

Vegetable risotto

225 g (8 oz) asparagus

1.25 litres (44 fl oz/5 cups) hot
  vegetable broth (page 12)

2 fresh artichokes

juice of half a lemon

4 tablespoons olive oil

1 small white onion, chopped

200 g (7 oz) zucchini
  (courgettes), sliced

150 g (5½ oz) fresh or
  frozen peas

250 g (9 oz) risotto rice

125 ml (4 fl oz/½ cup) white
  wine

30 g (1 oz) butter

3–4 tablespoons grated
  parmesan

2 tablespoons chopped parsley

flour, for coating

light olive oil

a handful of mint sprigs

The winning stroke here is the fried artichokes on top, as suggested by my friend Sergia. The combination of the artichokes & fresh mint to pull through the risotto as you are eating is truly great. When you are making your vegetable broth, be sure to add the trimmings from the asparagus to give a depth of flavour.

_Trim the asparagus & slice on the diagonal, leaving the tips whole. Add the trimmings to your vegetable broth as it simmers.

_To prepare your artichokes, trim away the outer leaves & cut a slice off the top. Halve the artichoke & remove the hairy choke if it has one, then cut each half into fine slices 4–5 mm thick. (*Keep them covered with cold water & a little lemon juice to prevent them turning black.*)

_Heat the olive oil in a wide pot & sauté the onion until well softened. Add the asparagus, zucchini & peas & sauté on high heat for a moment to just take the flavours. Add the rice, turning it through so it is well coated with oil. Season with salt & pepper, then add the wine & let that bubble away. Add 500 ml (17 fl oz/2 cups) of hot broth, lower the heat & simmer for about 10 minutes until much of the broth has been absorbed. Add another cupful of hot broth, stir in gently & then leave it to do its thing, adding another cupful of broth when necessary until the rice is tender & creamy (*about 20 minutes in total*). Don't let it get so dry that you have to keep stirring.

_Remove from the heat, then *mantecare* by adding the butter, parmesan & parsley & stirring gently. Add salt if needed.

_Just before your risotto is ready, drain the artichokes, pat dry & pat lightly in flour on both sides. Use a non-stick pan that will fit the artichokes in one layer if possible. Just cover the bottom with oil & heat up. Add the artichokes & fry until golden & crisp on both sides. Lift out onto a plate lined with kitchen paper to drain. Serve the risotto with a heap of hot fried artichokes on top, plus the fresh mint, extra parmesan & black pepper.

Serves 4

Risi e bisi

Rice & peas

900 g (2 lb) fresh peas, shelled
  or 450 g (1 lb) frozen peas
1.75 litres (59 fl oz/7 cups) hot
  vegetable broth (page 12)
12 thin slices cured unsmoked
  pancetta/rigatino (the
  peppery, salty one)
3 tablespoons olive oil
1 small white onion, chopped
2 tablespoons chopped parsley
250 g (9 oz) risotto rice
125 ml (4 fl oz/½ cup) white
  wine
1 tablespoon butter
2 tablespoons grated parmesan

This dish was traditionally good enough for the doges. It becomes an altogether different plate if you use shelled home-grown peas, & add the jackets to your broth as it simmers. If you are serving 6 you will want to have 4 more slices of pancetta to crisp up for the top. You could also add a fresh herb in here last minute.

__If you are using fresh peas, shell them & add the pods to your vegetable broth as it cooks.

__Chop 4 slices pancetta, reserving the rest for later. Heat the oil in a wide heavy-based saucepan or deep frying pan. Sauté the onion until golden & cooked through well. Add the chopped pancetta & cook briefly until softened. Add the peas & 1 tablespoon of the parsley & simmer for a minute. Add the rice & stir until it is well coated with the oil. Pour in the wine & let it bubble up for a few minutes to reduce the wine & mingle the flavours.

__When much of the wine has been absorbed, add 500 ml (17 fl oz/2 cups) of hot broth & continue cooking, stirring regularly & adding another 500 ml (17 fl oz/2 cups) more broth as it is absorbed, for about 20 minutes, or until the rice is tender. Check for seasoning. Just before the rice is cooked, add another 1 or 2 cupfuls of the broth & mix to make sure nothing is sticking. Taste for seasoning, but remember that you will be adding parmesan. Add the butter, the second tablespoon of chopped parsley & 2 tablespoons of parmesan & stir through. (*This should be a loose risotto, with some thick liquid running around the side, like a lovely soupy rice.*)

__Meanwhile, heat up a non-stick pan (*you shouldn't need any oil*) & fry the thin slices of pancetta until crisp & golden.

__Serve the risotto with black pepper & a good scattering of parmesan on top. Put a couple of slices of crisp pancetta on top of each serving & sprinkle with more parsley & grated parmesan or pecorino if you like.

Serves 4–6

Riso e patate

Rice & potatoes

Chicken broth:

2 x 325 g (11 oz) chicken leg
quarters
1 small onion, cut in half
1 carrot, cut in half
1 celery stalk with leaves,
cut in half
1 garlic clove, peeled but left
whole
1 bay leaf
1½ teaspoons salt

1 small leek, trimmed
3 tablespoons olive oil
280 g (10 oz) risotto rice
60 ml (2 fl oz/¼ cup) white
wine
480 g (1 lb 1 oz) potatoes,
peeled & cut into chunks
1 scant tablespoon finely
chopped rosemary
1 tablespoon butter
grated parmesan, to serve

Normally I don't go for double carbohydrate, but I really liked this & so did rest of the family. I made it with a chicken broth, which I loved, but you could use a vegetable broth for a lighter flavour. (If you prefer to use a pressure cooker you will only need to cook the broth for 20 minutes.)

You can cut the potatoes up small if you like, but I prefer just holding the potato in my hand & chipping this way & that to get irregular chips that can still fit on a fork/spoon/in the mouth. If you're preparing the potatoes in advance, put the pieces in a bowl & cover with cold water.

__Put all the broth ingredients in a large saucepan & pour in 1.75 litres (7 cups) of water. Bring to the boil, then lower the heat, partly cover & simmer for an hour or so. Remove the chicken pieces & vegetables from the broth, then strain into a bowl & skim off any fat from the surface. Keep warm. (*Make sandwiches with the chicken if you like.*)

__Slice the leek lengthways a few times & wash under running water. Pat dry & chop. Heat the oil in a wide heavy-based pan & sauté the leek until softened & lightly golden. Stir in the rice until well coated in the oil. Add the wine & stir until evaporated. Add the potato pieces & rosemary & stir well.

__Add 750 ml (26 fl oz/3 cups) of the warm chicken broth & simmer for about 10 minutes until most has been absorbed, then add another 500 ml (17 fl oz/2 cups) of broth & simmer for another 10 minutes.

__Add the final cupful of broth, stir & cook for a few more minutes until the risotto is quite soupy. Taste for seasoning & stir in the butter just before serving. Serve with parmesan & black pepper.

Serves 4–5

Risotto con le seccole

Risotto with meat

2 tablespoons olive oil
2 tablespoons butter
1 white onion, chopped
300 g (10½ oz) seccole
    (good-quality meat
    trimmings), finely chopped
250 ml (9 fl oz/1 cup)
    valpolicella or other red wine
about 1.25 litres (44 fl oz/
    5 cups) meat broth
280 g (10 oz) risotto rice
grated parmesan, to serve

I was surprised at how much I liked this. It is a wonderfully masculine dish. It's especially wonderful with the broth from Bollito di carne (page 227), but you can make it with a lighter meat or chicken broth or even vegetable broth. Traditionally, this was probably a very simple dish; by using good-quality red wine & broth from the bollito, this version becomes something quite noble. Seccole are the scraps of meat left attached to vertebra & bones — the trimmings. Here I have used the trimmings from top-quality cuts, like rump or sirloin steak.

__Heat the oil & butter in a wide heavy-based pan or a deep frying pan that has a lid. Sauté the onion until golden & well cooked through. Add the seccole & cook until all the liquid from the meat has evaporated & it starts browning & frying in the oil. Season with salt & pepper. Add the wine, let it bubble up & almost evaporate, then add 250 ml (9 fl oz/1 cup) of the broth. Cover with a lid & simmer on low for about an hour until the meat is tender & tasty & there is some thick sauce in the base of the pan (*check occasionally that nothing is sticking & add a little more broth or water if it seems necessary*).

__Add the rice & stir well. Add 500 ml (17 fl oz/2 cups) of hot broth & continue cooking, stirring regularly. Cook for about 20 minutes, or until the rice is tender, adding another 500 ml (17 fl oz/2 cups) when the broth has been absorbed. (*There should be enough salt in the broth but taste & see if you need to add extra.*) Stir in the remaining cupful of broth if it looks as if it's needed. The risotto should still have some liquid & the rice grains should be firm yet creamy.

__Take off the heat. Serve at once, with a good grating of parmesan & a grinding of black pepper.

Serves 4

Risotto di zucca

Pumpkin risotto

800 g (1 lb 12 oz) pumpkin

2 tablespoons olive oil

2 tablespoons butter

1 white onion, finely chopped

70 g (2½ oz) thick slice sweet
   pancetta without rind,
   chopped

1 sage sprig

a good pinch of peperoncino

250 g (9 oz) risotto rice

125 ml (4 fl oz/½ cup) white
   wine

1.25 litres (44 fl oz/5 cups) hot
   vegetable broth (page 12)

2 tablespoons grated parmesan

1 heaped tablespoon chopped
   parsley

You need to have a lovely sweet-tasting pumpkin here — the flavour of your pumpkin is what will make this so special. Pumpkin simmered with white onion is also often served as a contorno.

__Peel the pumpkin, remove the seeds & chop the flesh into 3 cm (1¼ inch) pieces. You should have about 600 g (1 lb 5 oz) of pumpkin pieces.

__Heat the oil & half the butter in a wide heavy-based saucepan or a deep frying pan that has a lid. Sauté the onion until golden. Add the pancetta & sage & cook briefly until softened — don't let the pancetta become crisp. Add the pumpkin pieces & season with a little salt & pepper & a good pinch of peperoncino. Cover with the lid & simmer, stirring once or twice, for 15 minutes or so until the pumpkin is tender & some of the cubes have collapsed & some kept their shape.

__Add the rice & stir well. Add the wine, lower the heat to a simmer & cook, stirring often, until almost all the liquid has evaporated. Add about 500 ml (17 fl oz/2 cups) of the broth & continue cooking, stirring regularly & adding more broth as it is absorbed, for about 20 minutes, or until the rice is tender. You may not need the final cupful of broth. The risotto should still have some liquid & the rice grains should be firm, yet soft & creamy.

__Add the remaining tablespoon of butter & the parmesan & parsley to the risotto. Remove the pan from the heat, stir with a wooden spoon or do the 'onda' & shake the pot to combine it well. Remove the sage sprig. Serve at once with a good twist of black pepper & scattering of parmesan.

Serves 4

ℛisotto al latte

Milk risotto

1.5 litres (52 fl oz/6 cups) milk
3 tablespoons olive oil
1 small onion or French shallot,
    peeled but left whole
300 g (10½ oz) risotto rice
a good grating of nutmeg
1 tablespoon unsalted butter
4 tablespoons grated parmesan

It's very important to serve this risotto as soon as it comes off the stove. Also, make sure you use a block of good parmesan that you grate yourself, not a pre-grated one from a packet — as you can see, there are so few ingredients in this simple risotto that you can't disguise any flavours. What you see is what you get. If you like, you could add a few blobs of a stronger cheese like gorgonzola at the end, but that is another thing altogether.

__Warm the milk in a pot.
__Heat the oil in a wide heavy-based saucepan or a deep frying pan. Sauté the whole onion to flavour the oil. Add the rice & stir well until it is coated in oil. Season with salt. Add half the warm milk, lower the heat to a simmer & cook, stirring often, until almost all the liquid has evaporated. Add another 2 cupfuls of the milk & continue cooking, stirring regularly, for 20 minutes or so in total, or until the rice is tender, adding the last of the milk towards the end to make a sloppy risotto. Taste that there is enough salt (*even though you will be adding parmesan, you will need enough salt here*). Remove the onion.
__Add a nice grating of nutmeg, the butter & parmesan & remove from the heat. Stir together. Serve at once with an extra heap of parmesan & a grating of black pepper.

Serves 4–6

&Risotto con la verza&

Risotto with cabbage

4 tablespoons olive oil

1 white onion, chopped

1 or 2 sausages (200 g/7 oz
   total), skinned & crumbled

750 g (1 lb 10 oz) cabbage,
   trimmed, core & outer leaves
   removed, thinly sliced

225 g (8 oz) risotto rice

1.5 litres (52 fl oz/6 cups) hot
   vegetable broth (page 12)

125 ml (4 fl oz/½ cup) white
   wine

30 g (1 oz) butter

3 tablespoons grated parmesan

The sausages here need to be pork ones like the Italian salsiccia that you can remove the casings from & then crumble the sausage meat. Make sure your broth is salted or then check the risotto well for seasoning, as there is a lot of cabbage added. I used savoy here – the cabbage can also be made as a side dish.

__Heat the oil in a wide heavy-based saucepan or deep frying pan that has a lid. Sauté the onion until softened, then add the sausage meat & cook until pale golden. Add the cabbage & some salt, then stir everything together, put the lid on & let it cook down, making sure nothing is sticking. Add 250 ml (9 fl oz/1 cup) of the hot broth, cover & simmer for another 20 minutes or so, stirring from time to time until tender. Taste for seasoning.

__Add the rice, stir well & then add the wine & cook until almost all the liquid has evaporated. Add about 500 ml (17 fl oz/2 cups) of the vegetable broth & continue cooking, stirring regularly & adding another 500 ml (17 fl oz/2 cups) broth when it is absorbed, for about 20 minutes, or until the rice is tender. About 5 minutes before the risotto is ready, stir in the remaining broth. The risotto should still have some liquid & the rice grains should be firm yet soft & creamy.

__Once the risotto is creamy & cooked with some thick liquid, lower the heat & stir in the butter & parmesan. Serve at once with extra parmesan & a grinding of black pepper over the top.

Serves 4–6

galoshes & *high-heels*

Today is cold, grey & raining. Flooding, actually. Men in hats & raincoats. Umbrellas everywhere & acqua alta. Galoshes & high heels. Mist. The canals are completely alive. We pass by the golden façade on the right. You would think you'd need to buy a ticket to look at that building, sparkling even on this watercoloured day.

IV

SECONDI

Mixed fried fish	Fritto misto di pesce
Mixed grilled fish	Grigliata mista di pesce
Monkfish with tomato	Coda di rospo al pomodoro
Liver & onions	Fegato alla veneziana
Baccala baked in milk	Baccala alla vincentina
Osso buco with rice & peas	Ossobuco con riso e piselli
Braised beef with amarone	Brasato con amarone di valpolicella
Squid stewed with ink	Seppie in nero con polenta
Fish with potatoes & mushrooms	Rombo con patate e funghi al forno
Fish fillets with artichokes	San pietro in padella con carciofi
Roast eel	Anguilla al forno
Eel with tomato	Anguilla in umido
Calamari with tuna mayonnaise	Calamari con salsa tonnata
Sausages & polenta	Luganega e polenta
Roasted guinea fowl with peverada	Faraona arrosto con la salsa peverada
Chicken in tomato	Pollo con pomodoro in tecia
Birds with polenta	Uccelli con polenta
Duck with anchovies & capers	Anatra in padella con acciughe e capperi
Pork in milk	Maiale al latte
Venetian sausage with beans	Musetto con fagioli piccanti
Pasta in broth	Pasta in brodo
Mixed boiled meats	Bollito di carne
Red pepper & anchovy sauce	Salsa piccante di peperone e acciughe
Aubergine in oil & vinegar	Melanzane sotto olio e aceto

Fritto misto di pesce

Mixed fried fish

8 calamari
light olive oil, for frying
8 scampi tails (red-claw,
   langoustines) or large prawns,
   peeled & deveined
2 small whole sole (about
   70 g/2½ oz each) or other
   small fish, cleaned & gutted
flour, for dusting
lemon, to serve, if you like

This is everywhere in Venice, featuring many different seafoods… sometimes with the tiny whole baby squid much appreciated by the Venetians. Eel is also appreciated, or you could use any fresh fish you like; sometimes vegetable sticks are on the platter, too. This is a combination I liked. Generally, the amounts for a fritto in Venice tend to be rather generous, but you can judge for yourself. I prefer to eat this for lunch rather than dinner & just have a salad on the table as well. Many Venetians say you don't need lemon here – they prefer to taste just the freshness of fish. You decide.

__To prepare the calamari, firmly pull the head & innards from the body & wash the body well. Cut off the head just below the eyes, leaving the tentacles in one piece if they're small. Discard the head, pull the transparent quill out of the body & rinse out the tube. Peel off the outer membrane & cut the tube into chunky rings, about 3–4 cm (1½ inches) thick.

__Heat enough oil in a large deep pan or wok to comfortably fry the fish. Pat all the seafood dry with kitchen paper, pat in flour & shake off the excess. Your oil must be HOT HOT before you add anything. Start with the sole (*they will take the longest to cook*) & a few calamari if they fit – once the sole are crisp & golden on both sides (& *cooked on the inside*) lift out with a slotted spoon onto a plate lined with kitchen paper.

__Add all the calamari to the pan, & the scampi too, if they fit. When golden, lift out to drain on more kitchen paper. Move to a dish (*lined with paper for serving, if necessary*).

__Serve with salt & black pepper… lemon for squeezing… cold white wine or prosecco. At once.

Serves 2

Grigliata mista di pesce

Mixed grilled fish

2 sole (about 200 g/7 oz each),
  cleaned & gutted
1 monkfish tail (about 600 g/
  1 lb 5 oz)
1 bream (about 350 g/12 oz),
  cleaned & gutted
4 scampi (red-claw, langoustines
  or large prawns), deveined
  but not peeled
4 large prawns, deveined but
  not peeled
4 small-ish squid or calamari,
  cleaned
1 garlic clove, peeled & halved
chopped parsley, olive oil &
  lemon, to serve

Here you can use any variety of small fish, perhaps snapper or bream. In Venice fish is often served on its own as a second course with very little done to it — just a sprinkling of parsley, lemon, olive oil, salt & pepper. This mixed fish grill is a rather grander situation. Add in scallops, or different fillets such as john dory, as you like. Eel, too, is also very much appreciated on the grill as it loses some of its fat — many people prefer it cooked this way to any other. You can be very flexible here, adding or doubling, leaving out, as you will… Here is what I used:

__Heat up your barbecue or chargrill. Clean the seafood if you are doing it yourself. Rub your serving platters with the cut garlic clove & sprinkle with a little parsley. Grill the seafood until cooked through & settle onto the plates with an immediate drizzling of olive oil & a sprinkling of salt & parsley (these will contribute to some juice on plate). Everyone can decide if they want more oil or lemon & ground pepper. Serve at once with a lovely salad & some bread.

Serves 4

Coda di rospo al pomodoro

Monkfish with tomato

1 monkfish tail (about 800 g/
 1 lb 12 oz) or 6 fish steaks
4 tablespoons olive oil
1 large onion, chopped
2 garlic cloves, chopped
375 g (13 oz/1½ cups) tomato
 passata
1 small peperoncino, crushed
125 ml (4 fl oz/½ cup) white
 wine
1 tablespoon chopped parsley
soft polenta, to serve (page 21)

This is a lovely, simple secondo that is easy to make in advance & then reheat just before the polenta is ready. If you have cooked the Pasticcio di pesce (page 128), this is perfect for using up the rest of the fish. But if you're just cooking this on its own, buy firm white fish steaks such as snapper, or any chunky cutlets.

___If you are using a whole monkfish tail, cut it into 6 or 7 steaks along the central bone, each steak about 3 cm (1¼ inches) thick.

___Heat the oil in a large frying pan with a lid & sauté the onion until well softened. Add the garlic &, when you can smell it, add the passata along with some salt, pepper & the peperoncino. Simmer, covered, for 10 minutes or so.

___Add the fish to the pan & sauté in the tomato, then turn over & briefly cook the other side. Sprinkle a little salt over the fish & add the wine. Once the wine has mostly bubbled away, lower the heat slightly, cover & simmer for about 15 minutes until cooked through. If the sauce is looking too dry, add a few tablespoons of water as necessary. Sprinkle with the parsley & serve with soft polenta.

Serves 4–6

Fegato alla Veneziana

Liver & onions

200 g (7 oz) calf liver
1 tablespoon butter
2 tablespoons olive oil
200 g (7 oz) white onion,
    halved & thinly sliced
a couple of sage sprigs
80 ml (2½ fl oz/⅓ cup) white
    wine
1 heaped tablespoon chopped
    parsley
soft or grilled polenta, to serve
    (page 21)

This is on every menu in Venice. You can easily double the recipe if you're serving more than a couple. Some people use 2 pans & cook the onions & liver separately, then unite them in one pan shortly before serving. The most important thing here is that the liver is top quality, so when it's cooked it should be very soft. Sergia adds a couple of unpeeled apple slices, too, to make the onions more 'digestible'. While it may not be very traditional, I like the sage in here.

__Wash the liver in cold water, pat dry & cut away any sinew. Slice into 2–3 mm (¹⁄₁₆–⅛ inch) pieces. Then cut more or less into triangles about 7 x 2 cm (2¾ x ¾ inches).

__Melt the butter in a large non-stick frying pan that has a lid, then add the oil. When hot, add the onion & cook, stirring, for a couple of minutes to get them going before adding the sage & a little salt. Cover & simmer over low heat for 15–20 minutes until soft & very pale golden. Add the wine if anything looks like it could be starting to catch or in the last 10 minutes or so. Stir often so nothing sticks.

__Take the lid off, move the onions to the side of the pan (*or remove to a plate*), turn the heat right up & add the liver. Cook for a couple of minutes until cooked through & just starting to change colour, turning halfway so both sides are browned. Once cooked, add salt & pepper (*& return the onions if you took them out of the pan*). Take the pan off the heat add the parsley. Serve at once with soft or grilled polenta.

Serves 2

Baccala alla vicentina

Baccala baked in milk

700 g (1 lb 9 oz) baccala
(salt cod), soaked
flour, for dusting
5 tablespoons olive oil
1 large white onion, halved
& thinly sliced
2 garlic cloves, chopped
about 6 large anchovy fillets in
olive oil, drained & broken
into pieces
2 tablespoons chopped parsley
750 ml (26 fl oz/3 cups) milk
a small handful halved, pitted
black or green olives, if
you like

*Lidia says that this is mainly served as a second course with grilled polenta &
grilled radicchio, so they have dolce (sweet), amaro (bitter) & polenta on the one
plate, which is a perfect combination. You need a baking dish that can also go on the
stovetop (mine measures 30 x 22 cm/12 x 8½ inches).*

*Before you use the salt cod you need to soak it to remove the excess salt. Rinse the
cod fillet first, then put it into a large bowl with enough water to completely immerse
them. Cover the bowl & refrigerate, changing the water 3–4 times a day. Ask your
fishmonger how long you need to soak the cod (it's usually 2–3 days). If you're
unsure, test the cod by breaking off a small fleck, rinsing & tasting it. The tail part
is always a bit more salty. In some places you can buy ready-soaked salt cod, which
is very reliable & convenient.*

__Preheat your oven to 180°C (350°F/Gas 4). Drain the baccala & break it
into 5 x 4 cm (2 x 1½ inches) pieces, discarding the skin & bones. Lay on a
tray, sift flour over both sides, then beat on your palm to get rid of the excess.
__Heat the oil in your flameproof baking dish & sauté the onion until
softened & pale gold. Add the garlic &, when you can smell it, add 3 of the
anchovies, squashing them into the onion so they almost 'melt'. Stir well, add
the parsley & arrange the baccala pieces on top, mixing so all the flavours get
mingled. Add 2 or 3 grinds of black pepper.
__Pour the milk into the dish, moving the baccala pieces so that the milk
seeps down. Add the rest of the anchovies. Cover the dish with foil & put in
the oven. Bake for about 1 hour, then uncover & cook for 30 minutes or until
the baccala & onion have drunk up almost all of the milk & there is a golden
crust on top. If you are using olives, scatter them over the top 10 minutes
before the end. Remove the dish from the oven & leave for the fish to finish
absorbing the rest of the liquid. If it seems too liquidy, return to the switched-
off oven (*the residual heat will help the fish absorb the milk more quickly*).

Serves 4

Ossobuco con riso e piselli

Osso buco with rice & peas

6 veal ossobuchi

flour, for dusting

2 tablespoons olive oil, plus
    4 tablespoons extra

100 g (3½ oz) celery, roughly
    chopped

100 g (3½ oz) carrot, roughly
    chopped

100 g (3½ oz) white onion,
    roughly chopped

2 garlic cloves, peeled but
    left whole

1 tablespoon finely chopped
    rosemary

250 ml (9 fl oz/1 cup) white
    wine

grated parmesan

Risotto:

1 tablespoon olive oil

1 tablespoon butter

½ white onion, finely chopped

300 g (10½ oz) risotto rice

125 ml (4 fl oz/½ cup) white
    wine

1.25 litres (44 fl oz/5 cups)
    vegetable broth (page 12)

This is a lovely piatto unico. The key to this recipe is to time the cooking so the risotto & peas are both ready as you take the ossobuco out of the oven… so start on the risotto about 30 minutes before the ossobuco is ready, & start the peas 10 minutes after you've begun cooking the risotto. Alternatively, cook the ossobuco at your leisure & then just heat through, adding a little water, when you want. I like to use vegetable broth for the risotto because it adds an extra dimension of flavour & takes little effort to make.

For the veal, you'll need a piece of shank that weighs about 1 kg (2 lb 4 oz), cut into 6 pieces. Each piece should be about 2 cm (¾ inch) thick & 10–12 cm (4 inches) in diameter, though it will depend on the size of the shank.

__Preheat your oven to 180°C (350°F/Gas 4). Snip the *ossobuchi* in a few places around the edge to prevent curling. Pat the meat dry with kitchen paper. Put onto a board & sprinkle with salt & pepper & then dust flour on each side. Shake off the excess flour.

__Heat the 2 tablespoons oil in a non-stick frying pan &, when the oil is hot, add the ossobuchi & fry for a few minutes on each side until golden & sealed.

__Meanwhile, pulse the celery, carrot & onion with the garlic in a food processor until evenly chopped. Heat the extra 4 tablespoons of oil in a flameproof casserole (about 30 x 25 cm/12 x 10 inches). Add the chopped vegetable mixture & put in the oven until the vegetables are softened, adding the rosemary to flavour for a few moments longer.

__Put the *ossobuchi* in a single layer on top of the vegetables in the dish. Sprinkle with a little salt, add the wine & 125 ml (4 fl oz/½ cup) water. Cover with foil & bake for 30 minutes. Turn the *ossobuchi* over gently so the meat holds its shape & doesn't lose any marrow. Cover & return to the oven for another 20–30 minutes or so (*this will depend on your oven*) until tender. Uncover & put back in the oven for about 30 minutes until the meat is lovely & tender & the sauce syrupy & not watery.

Peas:

1 tablespoon olive oil
½ white onion, peeled
20 g (¾ oz) slice of pancetta
1 garlic clove, peeled &
   squashed a bit
450 g (1 lb) frozen peas
2 scant tablespoons
   chopped parsley

__Meanwhile, make the risotto. Heat the oil & butter in a wide heavy-based saucepan or frying pan with high sides. Sauté the piece of onion until golden. Add the rice & stir until it is coated with the buttery oil. Season with salt & pepper. Add the wine, lower the heat to a simmer & cook, stirring often, until almost all the liquid has evaporated. Add about a cupful of the broth & continue cooking, stirring regularly & adding more broth as it is absorbed, for about 20 minutes until the rice is tender. The risotto should still have some liquid & the rice grains should be firm yet soft & creamy.

__While the risotto is cooking, cook the peas. Heat the oil in a saucepan & sauté the half onion (*still in one piece*), pancetta & garlic until it smells good. Add the peas, stir well, then add 1 tablespoon parsley, 125 ml (4 fl oz/½ cup) of water & some salt & pepper & simmer for about 15 minutes until the peas are tender but still a nice green. Remove the onion, pancetta & garlic clove. Drain the peas & scatter with the rest of the parsley.

__When everything is ready, serve the risotto, squashing the rice down a little, with the peas to one side & an ossobuco on top. Spoon on some of the lovely sauce & give a good scattering of grated parmesan & black pepper.

Serves 6

I keep feeling as if everyone is staring at me on the vaporetto. But — it is not me I realise. It is Venice. And the masterpieces everywhere, this show, this muchness of everything, everywhere.

Brasato con amarone di valpolicella

Braised beef with amarone

1.25 kg (2 lb 12 oz) chuck,
  blade or shin steak in one
  piece, trimmed of fat
4 tablespoons olive oil
2 carrots, halved
1 celery stalk, halved
1 white onion, halved
1 tablespoon butter
750 ml (26 fl oz/3 cups)
  amarone di valpolicella or
  other red wine
soft polenta, to serve (page 21)

Usually, the wine used in cooking would be the one to drink, but you may decide here to drink a great amarone & choose a less expensive bottle for cooking. Or a beautiful deep red wine instead. The cut of meat here is important as it has to become very soft. Ask your butcher to recommend a great piece of meat. I used La sfaldatura di bistecca dissosata, which is deboned steak & particularly good for a brasato. It is often made with shin of beef. A brasato (stew or braise) is usually cooked on the stovetop. Here I have started off the cooking on the stovetop & then finished it in the oven where you don't need to give it a glance for a couple of hours. Because the pot will be going from stovetop to oven it needs to be flameproof. I use my large cast-iron one with lid that is 30 cm (12 inches) across & almost as deep. Serve with a nice dollop of soft polenta.

__Preheat your oven to 180°C (350°F/Gas 4). Roughly tie the meat with kitchen string to hold its shape while cooking. Heat the oil in a flameproof casserole, add the meat & seal well on all sides until golden here & there. Season well with salt & pepper (this is important so that you don't get flavourless meat later). When the meat is almost browned all over, add the vegetables & butter & sauté so the vegetables get a bit of a colour.

__Add the wine &, once that starts bubbling, cover with the lid & put in the oven. Cook for 1 hour, then reduce the oven to 160°C (315°F/Gas 2–3) & cook for a further 1½ hours or until tender, turning once or twice.

__Lift the meat from the dish, remove the string & rest on a board while you finish the sauce. Use a hand-blender to purée the vegetables until smooth. You may need to cut the vegetables up a little first or add a little liquid from the pot to get a smooth purée.

__Cut the meat into 12 or so thick slices. Serve two or three slices of meat per person with a dollop of the sauce over the top & polenta on the side.

Serves 4–6

ℰ Seppie in nero con polenta

Squid stewed with ink

3 large squid (about 800 g/
   1 lb 12 oz total) with their
   ink sacs
3 tablespoons olive oil
2 garlic cloves, chopped
125 ml (4 fl oz/½ cup) white
   wine
400 g (14 oz) tinned crushed
   tomatoes
1 heaped tablespoon chopped
   parsley
a pinch of peperoncino
polenta (preferably white), to
   serve (page 21)

Squid stewed with ink is often made without the tomato; if you decide you'd like to make it that way, you may need to add an extra ½ cupful of wine & water so the sauce doesn't dry out. It can also be made as a primo, turned through spaghetti. The deep jet black colour of this dish is very dramatic & can deter timid diners, but the taste is wonderful. When I was cooking I couldn't see anything but black — I kept hoping that none of my rings would fall into the pot.

   If you're making slow-cooked polenta you'll need to start on it about the same time you start cooking the squid. If your squid doesn't come with ink sacs or if they don't yield much ink, you can supplement with a sachet of squid ink. These are sold by some fishmongers & delicatessens, usually in a package containing 2 sachets of 4 g (⅛ oz). Use one sachet & see how black the squid becomes before adding the other. Alternatively, you can make this without any squid ink at all — just don't tell people they are eating seppie in nero.

__To prepare the squid, pull the head & innards from the body. Separate the ink sac from the rest of the innards without puncturing it & then rinse gently & put in a bowl. Wash the body well. Cut off the head just below the eyes, leaving the tentacles in one piece, & discard the head. Pull out the transparent quill, rinse the tube & peel off the outer membrane. Cut the squid body & tentacles into chunks. Pat dry with kitchen paper.

__Heat the oil in a wide pan & add the squid. Cook over high heat until the liquid begins to evaporate & the squid turns golden on the bottom. Add the garlic, turning with a wooden spoon. When you can smell the garlic, add the wine & let that evaporate a bit.

__Cut the ink sacs into a cup & mix with 3 tablespoons of water, then add this to the pot. Add the chopped tomatoes, parsley, peperoncino & some salt & pepper. Cook for 5 minutes until it all starts bubbling up, then cover, lower the heat & simmer gently for about 40 minutes until the squid is tender & there is a good amount of sauce (*cook for longer, adding more liquid if necessary, until your squid is tender*).

__Check every now & then that nothing is sticking to the base of the pan. Add a little more water if it starts to thicken too much. Taste for seasoning.
__Put a generous mound of polenta on each plate, then top with a good dollop of squid. Scatter with extra parsley, if you like — or just leave it all stark black.

Serves 4

The vast open water highway makes me happy. To get on a quiet vaporetto & take a long ride away from the circus. Let my thoughts float out over the ripples of the water before they come back & settle into me again.

Rombo con patate e funghi al forno

Fish with potatoes & mushrooms

*about 820 g (1 lb 13 oz) whole
flat fish, such as turbot
or flounder*

*2 garlic cloves, peeled but
left whole*

1 thin bunch of parsley

coarse salt

4 tablespoons olive oil

*500 g (1 lb 2 oz) potatoes,
peeled*

*60 ml (2 fl oz/¼ cup) white
wine*

*300 g (10½ oz) fresh
mushrooms, porcini, field
or swiss browns, sliced*

*I love this method of cooking whole fish because it's so easy to do all your preparation
well ahead. You clean & prepare the fish & lay it in an oven dish with the oil &
salt, then put it in the fridge for a few hours until you're ready to cook it. During
this time the salt penetrates the fish. When you're ready, take it out of the fridge, add
the potatoes & pop it straight in the oven. If you're short of time, of course you don't
have to put it in the fridge, you can just cook it straight away. Don't overcook the
fish or it will lose its delicate softness &, once it's cooked, serve it straightaway.*

*This is lovely with or without the mushrooms, which are added 10–15 minutes
before the end of the cooking time. I use porcini here — I love the flavour they add.*

__Gut, clean & scale the fish but leave the head on (*your fishmonger can do
this for you*). Wash the whole fish & pat dry with kitchen paper. Stuff the fish
cavity with the garlic & parsley. Sprinkle in some coarse salt & pepper &
scatter some on the outside, too. Put the fish in a large oven dish. If you don't
think there will be room for the whole fish & the potatoes in your dish, cut
away the fins with a pair of kitchen scissors. Drizzle the oil into the bottom
of the dish. Cover with plastic wrap & put in the fridge for a couple of hours
to allow the salt to penetrate.

__Meanwhile, slice the potatoes into very thin rounds of 2 mm & keep them
covered in a bowl of water so they don't darken.

__Preheat your oven to 200°C (400°F/Gas 6) & remove the fish from the
fridge. Drain the potatoes & pat dry with kitchen paper. Scatter around the
fish in as flat a layer as possible. Put in the oven for about 15 minutes until
lightly golden. Drizzle the wine over the fish & pop back into the oven for
another 15 minutes (*by this stage the potatoes should be quite golden*). Sprinkle a
little fine salt over the potatoes, add the mushroom slices & season them with
a little extra salt & pepper. Cook for a final 10 minutes or so until everything
is cooked. When serving, carefully remove the fish skin & bones.

Serves 4

San pietro in padella con carciofi

Fish fillets with artichokes

2 fresh artichokes
juice of half a lemon
4 tablespoons olive oil
2 garlic cloves, peeled &
  squashed a bit
1 tablespoon chopped parsley
2 san pietro (john dory) fillets
  (about 200 g/7 oz each)
60 ml (2 fl oz/¼ cup) white
  wine

San pietro (john dory) is a very delicate fish & cooking for too long will cause it to break up. If you buy it whole & fillet it yourself, then use the head & trimmings to make a fish broth for risotto (page 159). Of course, you could use other firm white fish fillets here. If it's helpful to prepare the artichokes in advance, keep them in a bowl of cold water with a little lemon juice to prevent them discolouring.

__To prepare your artichokes, trim away the outer leaves & cut a slice off the top. Halve the artichoke & remove the hairy choke if it has one, then cut each half into fine slices 3–4 mm thick. (*Keep them covered with cold water & a little lemon juice to prevent them turning black.*)

__Heat half the oil in a frying pan. Add the artichokes & one of the garlic cloves & season with salt. Sauté gently for 5–10 minutes until softened & flavoured, then add the parsley & remove the garlic. Scrape out the artichokes onto a plate & wipe the pan clean.

__Meanwhile, pat the fish dry with kitchen paper. Heat the remaining oil & garlic clove in the frying pan & add the fish. Cook until just pale golden underneath, then turn over & add the wine. Lower the heat, shake the pan to loosen the fish & add salt & pepper. When the wine has bubbled up, add the artichokes to the side, turn off the heat & serve with a grind of pepper.

Serves 2

Anguilla al forno

Roast eel

8 eel fillets (about 900 g/2 lb)
5 tablespoons olive oil
dry breadcrumbs
3 bay leaves
2 garlic cloves, peeled but left
  whole
60 ml (2 fl oz/¼ cup) white
  wine
lemon wedges & grilled polenta
  (page 21), to serve

They say no one cooks eel like the Venetians do. You can make this with any oily fish fillets, such as hake, mackerel or mullet. I used mullet fillets & they worked beautifully. My father-in-law, Mario, loves eel — this is his recipe. If you're using eel, you can remove the skin if you prefer.

__Preheat the oven to 200°C (400°F/Gas 6). Cut the eel into pieces of about 6 x 8 cm (about 3 inches) & dry on kitchen paper. Drizzle 3 tablespoons olive oil into a good-sized roasting tin. Pat the eel in breadcrumbs, salt & pepper & arrange in the tin with the bay leaves & garlic. Drizzle with the remaining oil. __Roast for about 20 minutes or until golden, then add the wine & cook for another 5 minutes or so until it bubbles up & is saucy & roasty looking. Serve with lemon wedges & grilled polenta.

Serves 4

Anguilla in umido

Eel with tomato

about 3 tablespoons olive oil
1 onion, finely chopped
1 garlic clove, peeled but
    left whole
400 g (14 oz) tinned crushed
    tomatoes
8 eel fillets (about 900 g/2 lb)
flour, for dusting
60 ml (2 fl oz/¼ cup) white
    wine
2 tablespoons chopped parsley
soft polenta (page 21), to serve

You can make this with any oily fish fillets, such as hake, mackerel or mullet. Eel has a very distinctive flavour & there are people who love it & people who don't. Much eel is eaten in the Veneto, where it is known as bisato, & there are many different ways to prepare it. It has a delicate, slightly sweet taste & is also enjoyed fried & grilled. You can also sauté eel in a pan with butter, white wine, garlic & scatter with chopped parsley & serve with polenta.

__Heat 3 tablespoons oil in a large frying pan, add the onion & sauté to soften. Add the garlic &, when you can smell it, add the tomatoes & some salt & pepper & simmer for 10 minutes or so.

__Meanwhile, cut the eel into pieces of about 6 x 8 cm (about 3 inches). Dry the eel with kitchen paper & pat lightly in flour. Heat a little oil in another frying pan & fry the eel on both sides until lightly browned. Add salt & pepper, then pour away any oil from the pan before adding the wine. Let it bubble up & reduce.

__Scrape the whole panful of eel into the pan of tomatoes, add ½ cupful of water & simmer for 10–15 minutes, until nicely cooked. Add a little more water if it needs it. Sprinkle with parsley & serve hot with polenta.

Serves 4

Calamari con salsa tonnata

Calamari with tuna mayonnaise

4 calamari (about 450 g/1 lb)
95 g (3 oz) tin tuna in oil,
   drained
1 large tablespoon capers in
   vinegar, drained
3 tablespoons mayonnaise
   (below)
a little freshly chopped parsley
lemon wedges, to serve

Mayonnaise:
2 egg yolks
1 teaspoon lemon juice, plus
   1–2 extra teaspoons to taste
200 ml (7 fl oz) light olive oil

This recipe is a variation of Italy's famous Vitello tonnato. Someone told me about it on the island of Lido but using boiled squid or calamari, & I couldn't wait to try it. Here I've grilled the calamari, but you might like to try it boiled some time.

This is great. I've made it as a main, but it also works well for more people as an antipasto. You don't have to make your own mayonnaise — use a top-quality bought one. A lightly dressed salad is good with this.

__First make the mayonnaise. Whisk the yolks in a small bowl with a teaspoon of lemon juice & a pinch of salt. Dribble in the olive oil, whisking all the while, until the mayonnaise is thick & creamy. Add more lemon juice to taste. This makes about ¾ cupful (185 ml/6 fl oz) & will keep for a week in the fridge in a sterilised jar. You'll need 3 tablespoons of it for this recipe.
__To prepare the calamari, firmly pull the head & innards from the body & wash the body well. Cut off the head just below the eyes, leaving the tentacles in one piece if small. Discard the head, pull the transparent quill out of the body & rinse out the tube. Peel off the outer membrane & cut the tube down the length of one side, then open it out into a steak. Snip the edges & score the top with a sharp knife in slashes or a criss cross pattern.
__In a blender, pulse the tuna & capers until smooth-ish. Scrape out into a bowl & mix in 3 tablespoons mayonnaise. Taste & adjust the salt & pepper.
__Preheat your griddle pan to hot. Put the calamari steaks flat on the pan, with the tentacles, in a single layer (*or cook in batches*). Cook until deep golden so they take the taste of the grill pan, then turn & cook the other side until soft, tender, opaque white & with a few grill marks. They probably won't stay completely flat (*I held with tongs the parts that were threatening to curl*). Put flat on the plates. Let them cool a little (*too hot will melt the mayonnaise too much*) & cover with, say, a tablespoon of the salsa tonnata. Scatter with parsley & black pepper & serve at once with lemon wedges.

Serves 2

Luganega e polenta

Sausages & polenta

about 60 g (2¼ oz) thinly sliced pancetta, chopped

about 60 g (2¼ oz) thinly sliced lardo, chopped

6 good pork sausages (luganege) (about 650 g/1 lb 7 oz), pricked all over

1 small onion, sliced

250 ml (9 fl oz/1 cup) white wine

polenta (page 21) & grated parmesan, to serve

This is a simple & rich dish; the kind of thing you won't see on restaurant menus but that Venetians would make at home to eat in front of a wintery fire. Use good pork sausages, & I like to use a mixture of lardo & pancetta here. Lardo is rather a precious thing — 'lardo di colonnato' is a traditional Tuscan delicacy of cured pork fat & it is prized all over Italy. When sliced very thinly, the majority of the slice is pork fat with just a tiny piece of prosciutto-type meat. Pancetta is very well cured pork, much drier & with much more meat than lardo. Together they are a great combination. You'll need about 3 thin slices of lardo & 4 of pancetta. I use white wine here but red is also good. Serve this rich dish with polenta & perhaps a nice plate of radicchio or Verza soffogata (page 253).

__Sauté the pancetta & lardo in a dry frying pan over heat until some of the oil seeps out, then add the sausages. Cook the sausages until getting slightly golden in places. Remove the pancetta & lardo to a side plate so it won't become too crisp & add the onion to the pan. Cook until your onion is golden & soft (*your sausages might not yet look lovely & brown but they will have more time in the pan later*).

__Return the pancetta & lardo to the pan & fry for a few minutes until everything is nicely melded together. Add the wine & simmer for 30 minutes, turning the sausages over once until they are golden on the bottom, the wine has evaporated & things once again look as if they are frying in the oil. If you won't be serving immediately, cover with a lid. Serve a sausage & some of the sauce & rich oil over a serving of polenta. Scatter with parmesan.

Serves 6

&*Faraona arrosto con la salsa peverada*&

Roasted guinea fowl with peverada

*1 guinea fowl (mine weighed
  1.1 kg/2 lb 7 oz)*
1 tablespoon butter
*2 teaspoons finely chopped
  rosemary*
2 teaspoons finely chopped sage
1 large garlic clove, chopped
*30 g (1 oz) finely chopped
  pancetta*
5 long thin slices cured pancetta
4 tablespoons olive oil
*250 ml (9 fl oz/1 cup) white
  wine*

Salsa peverada:
80 g (3 oz) chicken livers
20 g (¾ oz) guinea fowl liver
*1 thick slice (80 g/3 oz) soft
  salami, skin removed, chopped*
2 tablespoons olive oil
*1 teaspoon finely grated
  lemon zest*
juice of 1 small lemon
2 garlic cloves, chopped
1 tablespoon chopped parsley

Serves 4

This is quite lovely, noble looking &, most of all, easy. It's rather like doing a roast chicken with a bit of a stuffing sauce on the side. Prepare as for a chicken, keeping the liver if your guinea fowl comes with one. This is particularly lovely with cabbage or the roast pumpkin & mushrooms (page 248). I have seen many different versions of this sauce; some elaborate with vinegar, crumbed bread, anchovies, onions or various spices, & it works very well next to any roast poultry. If your bird doesn't come with the liver just increase the chicken liver accordingly.

__Preheat your oven to 220°C (425°F/Gas 7). Rinse the guinea fowl inside & out & pat dry with kitchen paper. Season lightly inside & out. Mix together the butter, rosemary, sage, garlic & chopped pancetta & stuff inside the bird.
__Lay the sliced pancetta over the bird widthways so that the top & sides are covered & then tie up with string. Put half the oil in a roasting tin, put the bird in the tin & drizzle with the rest of the oil. Roast for 15 or so minutes until golden & sizzling on the bottom, then pour in half the wine. Turn the oven down to 180°C (350°F/Gas 4) & roast for another 40–45 minutes, adding the rest of the wine after say 30 minutes, once is bubbling nicely. Once or twice baste the bird with the pan juices. Poke a fork into the thickest part of the thigh & check the juices are clear (cook for 10–15 minutes more if needed, but it's important not to overcook it & dry it out). Leave to rest for 10 minutes before untying & cutting up into portions.
__Meanwile, make the peverada: clean the livers of any sinew then chop them well. Put all the ingredients in a small saucepan with salt & simmer for 10 minutes or so until the livers are cooked. Add a good couple of grinds of pepper. Serve a spoonful of this warm next to a portion of roast guinea fowl with its lovely pan juices.

Pollo con pomodoro in tecia

Chicken in tomato

1 x 1.25 kg (2 lb 12 oz)
    chicken, cut into 8 pieces
1 white onion, quartered
1 carrot
1 small celery stalk
1 garlic clove, peeled but
    left whole
4 tablespoons olive oil
1 tablespoon chopped parsley
1 tablespoon finely
    chopped rosemary
a good pinch of ground
    peperoncino
185 ml (6 fl oz/¾ cup) red
    wine
2 x 400 g (14 oz) tinned
    crushed tomatoes
polenta (page 21), to serve

I usually make this in my cast-iron pot. If possible, use an attractive pot that you can take straight to the table from the stove. The whole chicken, cooked until meltingly soft, has a wonderful flavour, but if you prefer absolutely no bones, then just use large chicken breasts.

There is a lot of tomatoey sauce here, which is lovely with polenta to soak it up. You can make your polenta the quick method or the 40 minute way — just make sure you allow enough time for it to be ready with the chicken. Or, make the chicken in advance & warm it up to serve just before your polenta is ready. Boiled or mashed potatoes or rice work well here, too.

__To prepare the chicken, remove the skin, fat & any stray bones. Put the onion, carrot, celery & garlic into a blender & pulse until roughly chopped but not too small.

__Heat the oil in your large pot & sauté the chopped vegetables & parsley until they start to smell good. Add the chicken & sauté until it changes colour & has browny bits here & there, turning so it cooks evenly.

__Add a generous amount of salt & pepper, then add the rosemary & peperoncino. Sauté to flavour well, then add the wine & cook to reduce a little. Add the tomatoes & let it all bubble up then simmer, partly covered, for about 1 hour, adding 250 ml (9 fl oz/1 cup) of water after about 40 minutes or when it starts to look as if it needs it. Taste the sauce & add salt & pepper if necessary.

__Meanwhile, get going on your polenta (*either the short or long way*) but keep in mind that it must be eaten as soon as it's ready. Leave the chicken covered (*lid completely on*) until you serve it… with a scattering of parsley if you like. Check carefully when you serve, for any small bones that may have come loose during the long cooking time.

Serves 4

Uccelli con polenta

Birds with polenta

12 small birds, cleaned, or
  6 small quail, halved
  & cleaned
12 long thin slices pancetta
30 g (1 oz) butter
2 tablespoons olive oil
60 g (2 oz) sweet pancetta,
  chopped
2 sage sprigs
185 ml (6 fl oz/¾ cup) white
  wine
polenta (page 21), to serve

In Venice small birds are used for this — tordi, merli or fringuelli. We used fringuelli which Mariella happened to have in her freezer. Ten small birds weighed 200 g (7 oz). You will probably find quail are more readily available, depending on where you live, but if you do use the small birds you'll only need to roast them for 30 minutes. I use slices of peppery pancetta for wrapping them.

__Heat the oven to 180°C (350°F/Gas 4). Salt & pepper lightly inside the birds, wrap each one with a slice of pancetta & secure with a toothpick.
__Heat the butter & oil in a small flameproof casserole & sauté the chopped pancetta & sage until the pancetta has melted. Add the birds in a single layer, sauté for a moment on both sides & then add the wine. Transfer the dish to the hot oven & roast for 30 minutes, or 50 minutes if you're using quail, until cooked & tender. Serve with soft polenta.

Serves 4

Anatra in padella con acciughe e capperi

Duck with anchovies & capers

*1 x 1.4 kg (3 lb) duck, cut into
8 pieces
1 white onion, chopped
30 g (1 oz) sweet pancetta,
chopped
6 large anchovy fillets in olive
oil, drained
2 tablespoons capers in
vinegar, drained
2 garlic cloves, chopped
2 teaspoons finely
chopped rosemary
2 teaspoons chopped sage leaves
375 ml (13 fl oz/1½ cups)
white wine*

*Cutting up a duck is not as easy as cutting up a chicken… so you might want to
ask your butcher to do it for you. Cut it in half first & then cut each half into four
pieces. If your duck looks terribly fatty then cut some of that away. You may need to
singe away any bits of feather, too — scrape away the remnants with a sharp knife.
You will need a large non-stick frying pan with high sides & a lid that fits well —
& even better if you can take it straight to the table for serving. This is lovely with
radicchio in padella & roast potatoes…*

__Dry-fry the duck pieces in a large non-stick frying pan until brown on all
sides, then season with salt & pepper (*not too much salt as you'll have anchovies
in the sauce*).
__Lift out the duck pieces to a plate & add the onion to the duck fat in the
pan. Cook until pale golden, then add the pancetta & anchovies, mashing
them into the oil with a wooden spoon. When they have melted & the
pancetta is softened, add the capers, garlic, rosemary & sage.
__When you can smell the garlic, return the duck to the pan & add the wine.
Put the lid on the pan & simmer for almost an hour, then add about 125 ml
(4 fl oz/½ cup) of water. Cook for another 20 minutes then remove the lid
& turn the duck pieces. Simmer for a further 10–15 minutes to get a glossy,
sticky sauce in the pan. The duck should be golden brown & very tender —
check with a fork.

Serves 4

&*Maiale al latte*&

Pork in milk

2 quite small fennels, trimmed
& halved lengthways
about 800 g (1 lb 12 oz) pork
loin, with only a little fat
on top
1 sage sprig
1 rosemary sprig
3 tablespoons olive oil
1 tablespoon butter
2 garlic cloves, peeled but
left whole
125 ml (4 fl oz/½ cup) white
wine
about 625 ml (21½ fl oz/
2½ cups) milk

The sauce may look as though it is curdled, but it tastes wonderful. If you really don't like the look of it, you can purée to render it smooth, but it is traditionally served as it is cooked. This is one of those dishes that does not reheat particularly well, so time it to be finished when you're ready to serve. You'll need a good big pot: large enough to fit the meat but not too wide, & leaving enough room for the fennel to be added later.

__Bring a small-ish pot of salted water to the boil. Add the fennel & boil for about 5 minutes until quite tender (*it will have more time in the pot later*). Remove with a slotted spoon to a plate. Cut the fennel halves in half again, leaving them attached at the base. Set aside for now.
__Tie up the loin piece with kitchen string, fastening the sage on one side & the rosemary on the other. Heat the oil & butter in your pan &, when it is fizzling, add the pork & cook until it is lovely & golden on all sides, adding the garlic towards the end of cooking so it doesn't burn. Once the pork is browned all over, season generously with salt & pepper (*this is important for the final flavour*).
__Pour in the wine & let it bubble up until there is a great-smelling syrupy juice in the bottom of the pan. Add 500 ml (17 fl oz/2 cups) of the milk. Bring to the boil, then lower the heat & simmer, covered, for about 1¼ hours, checking towards the end that the sauce is not evaporating too much. Carefully add the fennel around the meat, warm the rest of the milk & pour that in too. Sprinkle with a little salt if you think it needs it. Cook, uncovered, for another 15 minutes or until the pork & fennel are tender.
__Remove the pan from the heat & set aside for about 10 minutes, then lift the meat out of the sauce. Remove the string & cut the pork into fairly thick slices. Serve the pork & fennel with a generous helping of sauce & add a good grinding of black pepper.

Serves 4

Musetto con fagioli piccanti

Venetian sausage with beans

500 g (1 lb 2 oz) dried Lamon
   or borlotti beans
1 musetto (cotechino) sausage
   (about 600 g/1 lb 5 oz)
2 garlic cloves, peeled but left
   whole
1 sage sprig
4 tablespoons olive oil
1 white onion, chopped
50 g (1¾ oz) cured pancetta or
   rigatino, chopped
1 scant tablespoon finely
   chopped rosemary
2 pinches ground peperoncino
600 g (1 lb 5 oz) tinned
   crushed tomatoes

Musetto is a wintery Venetian dish — lovely in slices with a good dollop of mustard (Dijon is great), bread & a heap of the Veneto's beautiful taupy-red speckled Lamon beans. These beans are also a beauty with grilled salsiccia, or other sausages that you like — & if you can't find Lamon, just use borlotti beans.

Musetto is a Venetian sausage (also popular served with mashed potato or polenta), that I saw being kept in a separate warm broth to keep it soft & moist, then taken out with a long fork to slice as someone ordered a portion. I bought my musetto from my friend Sergia who has the alimentari there, & she gave me the full cooking instructions. Cotechino sausage is similar enough to use here, just larger across its diameter. If you can only find the precooked cotechino, follow the preparation instructions on the package.

__Soak the beans overnight in a bowl with plenty of water to cover.
__Stick about 8 toothpicks into the musetto & leave them in (*to let the fat come out during the cooking*), then put in a pot of water & bring to the boil. Partly cover the pan & boil gently for about 1½ — even 2 — hours, adding more water if necessary (*or follow the instructions on the packet if your cotechino is precooked*). Test with a fork to check that it is lovely & tender, then remove from the heat.
__Meanwhile, drain the beans, put in a big pot of fresh water with the garlic & sage & bring to the boil. Partly cover the pan & cook for anything from 30 to 50 minutes (*depending on your beans*) until tender but not too overcooked please (*they get another few minutes of cooking later*). Add some salt towards the end of their cooking time. Drain, keeping about a cup of the cooking liquid, & remove the garlic & sage.
__Meanwhile, heat the oil in a high wide pan & sauté the onion until it is soft & pale golden. Add the pancetta & sauté for a minute more, then add the rosemary & peperoncino. Add the tomatoes & a little salt & simmer for 10–15 minutes, punching the tomatoes down with a wooden spoon so the pieces dissolve.

__Add the beans to the pan & toss through gently without mashing them. Add about ½ cupful of the reserved bean water (*or more if it looks necessary*), & simmer for a few minutes to mingle all the flavours. Taste for salt & pepper & simmer for 5 minutes or so until it is all just right.

__Now… lift the musetto out of its cooking liquid &, if you are not serving it at once, you could keep it in a pot of warm vegetable broth so it stays tender, just as they do at Do Mori ciccheteria in Venice. Cut into slices about 1 cm (½ inch) thick, removing the skin, & serve with a heap of warm beans & your favourite mustard & bread.

Serves 6–8

Pasta in brodo

Pasta in broth

This is a primo, but fits here because it is lovely made with the complex meat broth from the bollito misto (opposite). Serve it before the bollito.

__If you are making pasta *in brodo* for 4 people, put about 1.5 litres (6 cups) of broth into a saucepan & bring to the boil. Check that your broth is well seasoned. Snap up 120 g (4 oz) of spaghetti (*break the strands into about 6 pieces*) & cook in boiling salted water until ready (*or you could use tortellini or tagliatelle instead*). Spoon into bowls, pour in the broth & serve with a generous scattering of parmesan.

Serves 4

Bollito di carne

Mixed boiled meats

425 g (15 oz) piece of tongue

½ boiling chicken (about 900 g/
  2 lb), rinsed

700 g (1 lb 9 oz) piece chuck
  steak or blade

440 g (15½ oz) oxtail (about
  3 thickish slices)

440 g (15½ oz) piece veal
  shoulder

400 g (14 oz) beef shin

1 large carrot, peeled

1 large onion, peeled

1 celery stalk

1 bunch of parsley

1 bay leaf

10 peppercorns

3 teaspoons salt

This is rather celebrational & Christmassy. Luisa says they serve this, then follow with a dessert of mascarpone, some more mostarda & baicoli biscuits. Serve the meats with the Salsa piccante di peperone e acciughe (overleaf) & some other accompaniments, such as fresh horseradish sauce & Mostarda (page 28).

The idea with this recipe is to cook the meats, then use the delicious broth that remains to make Pasta in broth (opposite) or a lovely meat risotto, such as Risotto con le seccole (page 172), & serve that as your primo or the next day. The mixed boiled meats are then served as the main course, & you can vary the cuts of meats to suit your tastes & needs. You'll need a large pot to make this — I have a 10 litre stockpot, but if you don't have such a large one, make a smaller batch.

__Put the tongue in a small pot & cover with salted water. Bring to the boil, then simmer, covered for about 1½ hours until tender (*it will cook for another hour later on, but needs to be cooked enough now to strip off the skin*). Drain, leave until cool enough to handle, then pull off the skin.

__Wash all the meat & pat dry with kitchen paper. Put the carrot, onion, celery, parsley, bay leaf, peppercorns & salt in your huge pot with 4 litres (16 cups) of water. Bring to the boil, then add the various meats. Return to the boil & simmer, covered, over a good heat so it's rolling gently but not bursting everywhere for about 1 hour. Add the tongue & cook for another hour. If necessary, top up with a bit more water. To check that the meat is ready, stick a fork into each cut & remove when tender (*the chicken may need to be removed before the other meats*). Remove from the heat & season with salt if you think it needs it.

__Serve at once or leave to cool a little. Carefully remove the meat to a warm serving dish, cut up & cover so it doesn't dry out. Strain the broth into a large bowl, then cover & refrigerate if you're not using it immediately. (*Once the broth sets you could remove the layer of fat on top.*)

Serves 6

Salsa piccante di peperone e acciughe

Red pepper & anchovy sauce

125 ml (4 fl oz/½ cup) olive oil

4 very large anchovy fillets in
  oil, drained

1 tablespoon flour

1 garlic clove, peeled & halved

200 g (7 oz) red pepper
  (capsicum), seeded & cut
  into pieces

1 tablespoon capers in
  vinegar, drained

185 ml (6 fl oz/¾ cup)
  vegetable broth, not too salty
  please (page 12)

2 teaspoons white wine vinegar

Luisa's grandmother always made this to serve with a bollito misto. You can also serve it with a simple plate of boiled chicken, fish or grilled meat. It's also great drizzled onto grilled bread.

__Heat the oil & anchovies in a small pot, whisking so the anchovies dissolve. Add the flour, whisking until smooth.
__Add the garlic, pepper & capers. Bring to a slow boil, then add the vegetable broth. Lower the heat & simmer for about 15 minutes, whisking now & then so nothing sticks. Cool a little then purée thoroughly. When completely cool, stir in the vinegar.

Makes 375 ml (13 fl oz/1½ cups)

Melanzane sotto olio e aceto

Aubergine in oil & vinegar

440 g (15 oz) long thin
  eggplants (aubergines)
1 tablespoon coarse salt
375 ml (13 fl oz/1½ cups)
  white wine vinegar
2 garlic cloves, peeled but
  left whole
2 bay leaves
a few peppercorns & whole
  peperoncini, if you like
about 250 ml (9 fl oz/1 cup)
  good olive oil

These eggplant pickles are lovely to eat with the bollito (page 227) or even as part of an antipasto. You need to use the long, slender eggplants here (about 2 or 3 should make up the weight) so you'll get strips with the skin & not have too many pieces that are just flesh. You might like to add a couple of dried peperoncini or peppercorns to the container when packing the eggplant pieces in oil. The eggplant will keep for a month or longer as long as it's covered with oil. The container (glass or ceramic) must be cleaned & then sterilised with boiling water before use. Leave it to dry in a warm oven.

__Cut the eggplants into 2 cm (¾ inch) thick slices along their length. Then cut across those slices into 1 cm (½ inch) pieces. Put in a colander, scatter with the salt & leave in the sink or in a larger bowl for an hour or so.
__Put the vinegar & 250 ml (9 fl oz/1 cup) of water in a pot & bring to the boil. Rinse the eggplants, shake well, then tip into the vinegar. When the liquid comes back to the boil, lower the heat slightly & cook for 4–5 minutes — no more. Remove from the heat, lift out the eggplant with a slotted spoon & leave to cool in the colander. (*You can keep the lovely vinegar if you think you might make more eggplant pickles over the next few days.*)
__When cool, pack the eggplant into a sterilised container with the garlic & bay leaves. Add a few peppercorns and peperoncini, if you like. Cover with the oil (*the amount you need will depend on your container*). Press down on the eggplant to make sure there are no air bubbles. Seal. Leave for a couple of days before eating. Serve with some of the oil in a bowl on the side.

Serves 6–8

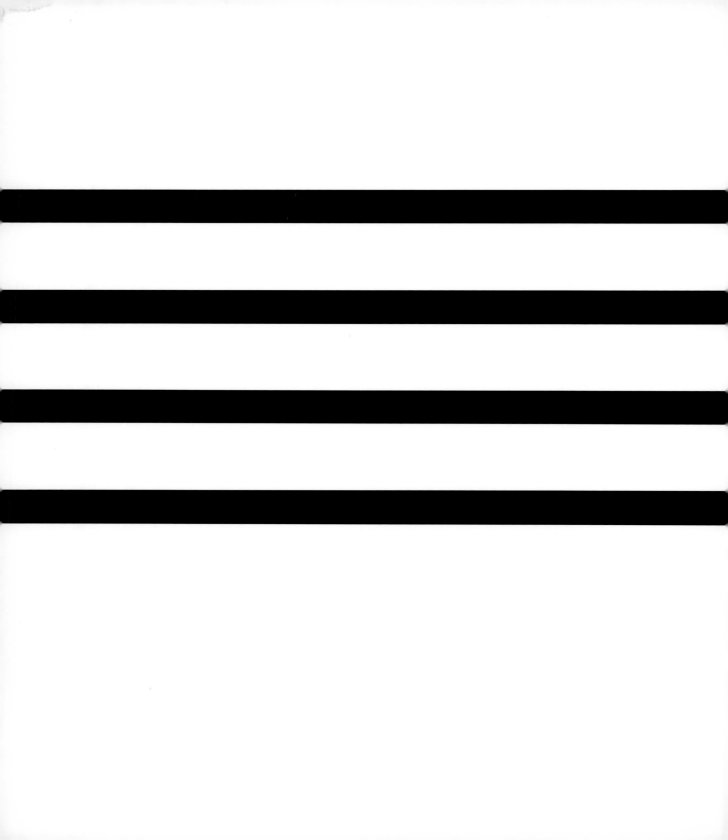

radicchio & roses

I love Pellestrina & its slow sadness. After sgroppinos & tiramisu, at that same round table at the entrance where the ladies had been peeling miniature prawns & were now cracking cooked crabs , I ask if they'll give me the recipe. They say, PER UN CURIOSO CI VUOLE UN BUGIARDO – FOR A CURIOUS PERSON ONE NEEDS A LIAR ! *Our friend, whom we have just met over lunch, takes us back on his jeanneau. His son Sebastian, aged seven, knows a lot. He tells me there is fresh thyme in the pasticcio. They told him so once.* ⤙

VII

CONTORNI

&*Castraure in padella*&

Tiny whole artichokes

about 25 castraure
juice of half a lemon
2 garlic cloves, chopped
4 tablespoons olive oil
2 tablespoons chopped parsley

Castraure are beauties — the small bitter first artichokes that bud on the island of Sant' Erasmus (a nice vaporetto ride from the fondamenta Nuova). They are considered a prize & are much appreciated — so small & perfect that it is not necessary to take out a choke. Make as many as will fit in a large non-stick frying pan (I have said about 25 here but yours may be of a different size). If you don't have castraure, use ordinary artichokes, quartered. Or baby artichokes. If you have some vegetable broth then definitely use that instead of the water here, please.

__Remove the outer leaves of the castraure & cut off all but 2 cm (¾ inch) of the stems. Cut off the outer bitter dark green bit. Cut off the tops, about a third of the way down. As you prepare them, drop the castraure into a bowl of water with the lemon juice added to prevent them discolouring.

__Heat the garlic & olive oil in non-stick frying pan & add the drained castraure in a single layer. Cook until you can smell the garlic. Add the parsley, turn through & season with salt & a grind of black pepper. Add about ½ cupful of water, cover the pan & simmer over low heat for about 10 minutes.

__Take off the lid & turn up the heat a touch & simmer for another few minutes until the water has all gone & just the oil is left in a bit of sauce at the bottom. Serve warm or at room temperature, with the remaining oil poured over, & a squeeze of lemon & black pepper if you like.

Serves 5–6

Fondi di carciofo

Artichoke bottoms

8 artichokes
juice of half a lemon
1 garlic clove, chopped
1 tablespoon chopped parsley
3 tablespoons olive oil

These are everywhere. I believe many Venetians buy the frisbee-sized artichoke bottoms ready prepared that I have seen in abundance in the Rialto market. The first outer tough leaves can be thrown away. The next layer of leaves can be saved in a bowl with water & lemon juice. Drain them later & dip the tips in a ramekin of olive oil, lemon, salt & pepper & scrape off with your teeth. The softer inner leaves & all trimmings can go into a vegetable soup or salad.

Use the bigger, wider variety of artichokes if possible. You can make many more of these in your pan — as many as will fill it, depending on their size.

__Cut away the stalk of the artichoke leaving only a couple of centimetres. Now cut that piece off & trim away the outer bitter parts to get to the inner core. (*These can go into a soup.*) The bottoms of the artichokes here need to be flat but the first inner stem bit is good, so save that. Cut away the first couple of centimetres off the top so that it is flat. Now pull away the first tough leaves & discard.

__Next layer the leaves to be saved in a bowl of water with the lemon juice added. The leaves which are still a bit hard but can be eaten in pinzimonio (*raw, dipped in lemon & olive oil*). Then get to the inner bits & trimmings & pop them into the soup pot. If the choke is hairy, cut it away with a small knife or pointed spoon & just have the bottom. If you are not ready to cook them, keep them in lemon water for now.

__Have a pot of broth or water boiling, add the artichoke bottoms and boil gently for 5–10 minutes, or until tender, then lift out with a slotted spoon.

__Heat the oil in a non-stick pan. Add the artichokes & sauté for 2 minutes over high heat to give a nice colour to both sides. Then add the garlic & turn through until you can smell it, season & add the parsley. Cover with a lid & cook for a few moments until the artichokes are tender. Leave the lid on until you serve, with some of the parsley garlic oil dribbled over.

Serves 4–8

ℰRadicchio con acciughe

Radicchio with anchovies

1 large radicchio di Treviso
    (about 250 g/9 oz), halved
    lengthways
2 tablespoons olive oil
1 large garlic clove, peeled &
    squashed a bit
4 large anchovy fillets in oil,
    drained
1 heaped tablespoon capers,
    drained
1 brimming tablespoon red
    wine vinegar

*This is quite definite in flavour – yet with a delicate dressing. Mix through well &
taste before adding anything more to your plate.*

__Slice the radicchio into 1–2 cm (¾ inch) thick easy-to-eat slices, discarding
the tough white stalk. Wash well, drain & arrange over a platter.
__Heat the olive oil, garlic clove & the anchovies in a small pan over very
gentle heat, mashing the anchovies with a fork until dissolved. Remove the
pan from the heat & stir in the capers. Cool a little, stirring with a wooden
spoon. Remove the garlic clove.
__Drizzle the flavoured oil over the radicchio. Add the vinegar to the
saucepan, swirling it around to gather all the pan flavours then drizzle it over
the radicchio. Take the platter to the table or dish up onto individual plates.
Serve immediately with a good twist of black pepper & some bread.
Beautiful simplicity.

Serves 2–3

Radicchio al limone

Radicchio in lemon

3–4 small or 2 large radicchio
di Treviso
5 tablespoons olive oil
juice of 1 large lemon

Nice. Bitter. Easy. This is great when radicchio is in season & is a lovely side dish with the liver & onions (page 190) or any secondo you think would go well. Apart from being such a gorgeous colour, radicchio is also very good for us. You need the longer Treviso radicchio for this — the round puffy ones are from nearby bustling Chioggia. With any luck all your radicchio will be similar inside — but the ones with a lot of 'anima' (the white stem) will need to be left over the heat a while longer. It's important that they are soft but not collapsing & are nice & crusty from the cooking. When you cut them, leave the leaves attached at the stem — some leaves may fall away but you will serve them intact. For a spicy kick, add some crumbled peperoncino to the pan. You can make radicchio al vino rosso by using 80 ml (2¾ fl oz/⅓ cup) of red wine instead of the lemon juice.

__You will need a large, good-quality non-stick frying pan that has a lid. Halve or quarter the radicchio, depending on the size, so they fit in your pan in a single layer. Trim away any hard outer leaves if necessary but leave the leaves attached to the stem. Wash the base. Pat dry with kitchen paper.
__Heat the oil in your pan, add the radicchio pieces, cut-side down, & sauté over high heat until the bottoms are cooked & golden. Gently turn over & cook for a few moments to get the underside going, then sprinkle with some salt & pepper & pour over the lemon juice.
__Put the lid on, lower the heat to medium & simmer for about 10 minutes until the radicchio is soft but still attached at the stems & there is some pink syrupy sauce in the pan. The base of the radicchio should be crusty here & the leaves should be soft & delicious. Cook for longer & add a little more liquid if necessary. Sprinkle a little more salt (& *some pepper, if you like*) over the top. Best served warm but also good at room temperature.

Serves 4–6

Zucca e funghi al forno

Roast pumpkin & mushrooms

800 g (1 lb 12 oz) pumpkin
5 tablespoons olive oil
about 400 g (14 oz) fresh
   porcini or field or swiss
   brown mushrooms, cut
   into chunks
2 garlic cloves, chopped
1 tablespoon finely
   chopped rosemary
about 3 tablespoons grated
   parmesan

This is Luisa's dish. It's a beauty — simple & lovely. You can make it ahead of time & pop it into a hot oven to reheat for a moment just before serving. I tend to use my round 30 cm (12 inch) baking dish to make this but you could use a rectangular one of about 26 x 23 cm (10½ x 9 inches), about 5 cm (2 inches) deep. You can easily add more pumpkin & mushrooms here — just fill up your dish.

__Preheat your oven to 180°C (350°F/Gas 4). Peel the pumpkin, remove the seeds & cut the flesh into 5 mm (¼ inch) slices. You should have about 600 g (1 lb 5 oz) pumpkin slices.
__Drizzle some of the olive oil into your baking dish. Add the pumpkin slices, mushrooms, garlic & rosemary & season with salt & pepper, then drizzle over the rest of the olive oil. Turn well using your hands or a wooden spoon, then spread everything out more or less rustically.
__Bake for 30–40 minutes until the pumpkin is tender & golden in places & the mushrooms are crisp & golden here & there. Scatter with parmesan & bake for another 5 or 10 minutes. Serve warm or even at room temperature.

Serves 4–6

～La peperonata～

Peppers

2 red & 1 yellow quite large
   peppers (capsicums)
   (about 1 kg/2 lb 4 oz)
about 5 tablespoons olive oil
1 white onion, chopped
2 garlic cloves, chopped
about 3 tablespoons white
   wine vinegar
3–4 anchovy fillets in
   oil, drained
a small handful of small capers
   in vinegar, drained
2 tablespoons chopped parsley

This is a classic dish using peppers. There are several variations on the recipe: some cooks add tomato or aubergine (eggplant), some use no anchovies & capers, some just red peppers. I love it with the capers & anchovies. It's lovely warm or even cold from the fridge (as Giovanni likes it) & is great on toasted bread. This is one of those beautiful dishes where you can taste every ingredient.

___Rinse & dry the peppers, then remove the seeds & stem & cut the flesh into nice rustic chunks.

___Heat the oil in a large frying pan & sauté the onion until soft & turning golden here & there. Add the peppers & cook on a strong simmer until they get going well. Add a tiny amount of salt (*you will be adding anchovies later*). Stir in the garlic, then put a lid on the pan & simmer for about 15 minutes until the peppers have surrendered their firmness — a bit gold in places is good. Stir with a wooden spoon now & then to check that nothing gets stuck but there should be enough liquid created from the peppers.

___Splash in the vinegar & simmer uncovered for another 10 minutes or until it has all joined in a syrupy way in the bottom of the pan & looks good.

___Add the anchovies to a bare space in the sauce in the bottom of the pan, mashing them to dissolve, then mix well & simmer for a few minutes more. Add the capers, parsley & some black pepper & turn through before removing from the heat.

Serves 6

Asparagi selvatici di Lidia

Lidia's wild asparagus

about 1 kg (2 lb 4 oz) thin wild
  asparagus (or the thinnest
  asparagus you can buy)
750 ml (26 fl oz/3 cups) white
  vinegar
250 ml (9 fl oz/1 cup) red
  wine
2 teaspoons salt
plenty of olive oil
2 garlic cloves, peeled & halved
about 12 whole peppercorns

Lidia used to collect the long thin wild asparagus on an island of the lagoon called Caroman. She would pick it by hand at the edge of the small wood, where it grew in the sand – long, long & thin, thin.

We cooked the asparagus in 2 batches in a frying pan large enough to fit them lying flat. But if you don't have a large (or very tall) pan, you can do it in a smaller pan & in several batches as long as they are all cooked in the vinegar equally. If your asparagus is of normal thickness, you can still make this but cook it in the vinegar for a minute or two longer. You'll need a tall container to store the asparagus; it must be first cleaned, then sterilised with boiling water & left to dry in a warm oven.

It may seem a lot of oil but the flavour is wonderful – it is great drizzled over salads, boiled potatoes & rice salads.

__Snap off the tough ends of the asparagus, then wash the stalks. Heat the vinegar, red wine & salt in a large frying pan or a tall pot. Bring to the boil. Add the asparagus, in batches if necessary, so they are immersed in the vinegar. Bring back to the boil & boil for 2–3 minutes, depending on the thickness of the asparagus

__You won't need the lovely pink vinegar here, but you can save it for cooking another batch, so drain the asparagus, then lay it out onto a clean cloth to cool & dry thoroughly. When cold, take a tall sterilised jar that will fit all the stalks (*or a rectangular dish*) & pour in a cupful of olive oil. Pack in the garlic, peppercorns & asparagus & add anther cup of oil, or enough to cover the asparagus completely. Sprinkle the tops with a little more salt.

__Leave for a few days before eating, as is, or with salads, rice salads or cold pasta. These get better with time & will keep well for a month if the asparagus is immersed in the oil.

Serves many

La verza soffogata

Suffocated cabbage

about 750 g (1 lb 10 oz) whole
  savoy cabbage
3 tablespoons olive oil
1 white onion, thinly sliced
125 ml (4 fl oz/½ cup) white
  wine
about 3 tablespoons tomato
  passata
a pinch of peperoncino

This is a great accompaniment for the Luganega e polenta (page 215) or just some sausages & lovely bread. Savoy is great here but you can use any type of cabbage. Remove a few of the darker, tougher outer leaves to use in a soup — it helps if most of your leaves are similarly tender so the cooking times don't differ too much, although it is also nice to have some variation in texture. I have also tasted this with a little splash of vinegar, which must have been added with the wine.

__Rinse the cabbage & divide into quarters lengthways. Cut away the hard bottom stalk in a triangle shape. Cut the cabbage into 8 mm thick slices.
__Heat the oil in a large non-stick saucepan & gently sauté the onion until pale golden & softened. Add the cabbage, some salt & cook, covered, until the volume reduces & the bottom is pale gold, then add the wine & allow it to bubble for a minute or so without the lid. Add the tomato passata, peperoncino & 500 ml (17 fl oz/2 cups) of water. Bring back to the boil, cover, lower the heat & simmer gently for about 30 minutes, turning through now & then with a wooden spoon to check nothing is sticking.
__Take the lid off & cook for another 10 minutes or so on a higher heat so that the liquid almost completely evaporates. If the cabbage is still hard, carry on cooking for a little longer — adding a little more water if it needs it — until the cabbage is meltingly soft & tastes quite sweet. Remove from the heat. Taste for seasoning. This is best warm but is also good at room temperature.

Serves 6

sweets & secrets

*Waiting in the line of cars to get onto the ferry to leave, I ask the taxi driver in front what's going on. Unless they bring a second boat we won't get on — there are too many, he says quite casually. I glance at my watch. So, if we don't make this one we will get on the 11.40, he says rather calmly, as I panic & ask him how this is possible. 'Eh, eh' he says, we Venetians are used to it. If you didn't book for the fast line, then that's how it is. When you live with the sea you have to be calm. The water is slow but inexorable. Is that a Venetian saying? I ask him. Not exactly, he says, but there are many similar. The Venetians are pensive & elusive at once, accepting, like the tides of their waters. *

VIII

DOLCI

Tiramisu	Tiramisù
Sergia's tiramisu	Tiramisù di Sergia
Mascarpone cream	Crema di mascarpone
Polenta biscuits	Zaletti
Crisp biscuits	Baicoli
Amaretti tart	Torta di amaretti
Lemon ice cream	Gelato al limone
Lemon chill	Sgroppino
Crumbler cake	Sbriciolona
Cooked apples with amaretti	Mele cotte con amaretti
Amaretto ice cream	Gelato di amaretto
Eggs and marsala	Zabaione
Zabaione ice cream	Gelato di zabaione
'S' or round biscuits	Bussola
Venetian focaccia	Focaccia veneziana

~Tiramisù~

3 fresh fresh eggs, preferably organic, separated
3 heaped tablespoons sugar
250 g (9 oz) mascarpone
about 125 ml (4 fl oz/½ cup) strong coffee
about 3 tablespoons rum, cognac or kirsch
about 30 pavesini or small savoiardi biscuits
unsweetened cocoa powder, for dusting

This can be varied as much as you like: make it less sweet, more sweet; serve it with gratings of dark chocolate on the top; use whatever alcohol you like, such as grand marnier, whisky or marsala. It's also very easy to make double the amount.

My friend Claudia makes this for the children with no alcohol. She mixes milk in with the coffee for a lighter version.

You can either make this in individual dishes or one large one. Small dishes need to be about 5 cm (2 inches) high & long enough across the base to fit the biscuits, so at least 7 cm (2¾ inches). I prefer individual ones but if you'd like to make this in one large dish, it should be about 26 x 18 cm (10 x 7 inches) & 5 cm (2 inches) deep. Mine is slightly wider at the top so I usually have to add more biscuits to the top layer than I did to the bottom.

__Whip the egg whites until very fluffy & white. Next, (*you don't need to wash the beaters*) whip the egg yolks & sugar for an age in a bowl until it is as creamy as you think it will ever get. Mix in the mascarpone & give a quick whisk, then fold in the egg white until lovely, full & *voluminoso*.

__Make your coffee (*if you're using a moka, listen for the beautiful 'ready' sound*). Pour the coffee into a bowl (*if you like, stir in 1 teaspoon of sugar to sweeten it*). Allow to cool a little, then splash in your alcohol.

__Have your 6 dishes ready & dollop a tablespoon of marscarpone into each bowl. Dip a couple of biscuits at a time into the coffee until they have soaked it up, then shake them out well so any excess coffee drips back into the bowl & you don't end up with soggy biscuits. Lay the biscuits over the mascarpone in the bowl. Top with another couple of dollops of mascarpone, then more biscuits, then a final couple of dollops of mascarpone – don't go all the way to the top of your dishes. Put them on a tray in the fridge for at least a couple of hours & dust with cocoa before serving.

__If you are making the tiramisù in 1 large dish, dollop about 3 tablespoons of the mascarpone mix into the dish & smudge it to just cover the bottom so the biscuits will stick. Arrange a layer of dipped biscuits like 2 rows of soldiers facing each other (about 8 per row). Dollop about half of the mascarpone cream over this layer, then another layer of biscuits, & the rest of mascarpone. Cover with plastic wrap & chill for at least a couple of hours & dust with cocoa before serving.

Serves 6

&*Tiramisù di Sergia*&

Sergia's tiramisu

15 *small amaretti biscuits,*
  plus 3 extra, if you like
3 *tablespoons Martini*
  Rosso (sweet vermouth)
1 *egg, separated*
1 *heaped tablespoon sugar*
200 *g (7 oz) mascarpone*
unsweetened cocoa powder,
  for dusting

Sergia taught me this recipe — a lovely bittersweet variation on a classic — which is so very quick to make. It has less biscuit & doesn't involve the layering of a traditional tiramisu. Make sure you have elegant glasses on a stem for serving. This recipe only makes a small amount, perfect for filling 3 of my lovely stemmed glasses, but you can easily double the quantities if necessary.

__Into each of 3 glasses put 5 amaretti, laying them as flat as you can. Splash the amaretti with a tablespoon of vermouth & leave for the liquid to be absorbed by the biscuits.

__Meanwhile, whip the egg white until very fluffy & white. Next (*you don't need to wash the beaters*) whip the egg yolk & the sugar very well in a bowl (*not too big*) until it is as creamy as you think it will ever get. Mix in the mascarpone & give a quick whisk, then fold in the egg white until lovely, full & *voluminoso*.

__Dollop the cream into the glasses (*you are just having one layer here*). Cover with plastic wrap & put in the fridge for a couple of hours. When you are ready to serve, add another biscuit to the top of each glass if you like (*it is good for scooping up the mascarpone*) & add a generous sifting of cocoa powder.

Serves 3

Crema di mascarpone

Mascarpone cream

2 egg yolks
1½ tablespoons sugar
4 drops vanilla extract
200 g (7 oz) mascarpone
a couple of good pinches of
   ground cinnamon
1 tablespoon brandy
baicoli (page 264) or hard
   biscuits, to serve

Serve this in a small bowl or ramekin with a pile of baicoli (page 264) stacked up like dominoes — this is how I ate it in Venice. Or serve with other biscuits that you can use as the spoon. You can use another liqueur such as rum or grappa or a mixture, if you like.

__Use electric beaters to beat the yolks, sugar & vanilla until as creamy & firm as possible (*very important*).
__Quickly whisk in the mascarpone & cinnamon until well incorporated. Then add the brandy to loosen it slightly to a lovely cream. Dollop into four ramekins. Cover with plastic & put in the fridge for at least an hour before serving, so that the cream isn't droopy. Serve with baicoli or similar biscuits.

Makes 4 gracious servings

There is still time to admire the water in front before the boat arrives & listen to the fisherman. A boatman clanking on a nail with a hammer. A couple of ladies swapping remedies while the wind is lifting. Just another day in beautiful Venice.

~Zaletti~

Polenta biscuits

70 g (2½ oz) sultanas
2 tablespoons grappa or brandy
125 g (4½ oz) unsalted butter
100 g (3½ oz) sugar
1 teaspoon vanilla extract
1 egg, plus 1 egg yolk
a pinch of salt
150 g (5½ oz) cake (00) flour
150 g (5½ oz/1 cup) fine
  yellow polenta
1 teaspoon baking powder
30 g (1 oz) pine nuts

These are lovely tasting & lovely textured, with a good crispness even among their softness, on account of the polenta. I have seen many versions & many various sizes.

__Soak the sultanas in the grappa or brandy. Meanwhile, use electric beaters to cream the butter, sugar & vanilla until creamy. Beat in the eggs & salt. Add the combined flour, polenta & baking powder & mix together with a wooden spoon to get a not-too-solid paste. Pour in the sultanas & grappa & the pine nuts & work them into the mixture.
__Cover & refrigerate the dough for about 30 minutes until it is firm.
__Preheat your oven to 170°C (325°F/Gas 3). Line 2 baking trays with baking paper. Remove the dough from the fridge & put it on a floured work surface, then divide it into two *salami* about 4 cm (1½ inches) in diameter. Cut into 1 cm (½ inch) thick discs, then shape these into 'lozenges' about 7 cm (2¾ inches) long.
__Put the biscuits on the baking trays, leaving room for them to spread. Bake for about 15 minutes until firm & lightly coloured. Cool on a wire rack, then store in an airtight container.

Makes about 40

Baicoli

Crisp biscuits

1 tablespoon dried yeast or
   15 g (½ oz) fresh
185 ml (6 fl oz/¾ cup) warm
   milk
200 g (7 oz) unsalted butter,
   softened
80 g (2¾ oz) sugar
about 500 g (1 lb 2 oz/4 cups)
   cake (00) flour, plus a
   little extra
1 egg white
a pinch of salt

I fiddled with a couple of recipes & ended up liking this one, even though it is quite different to actual baicoli. But everyone I asked in Venice said they had never & would never make their own, but of course they can just pop down to any shop to buy them, so why would they? Anyway, yours will not be the same as the manufactured types so expect a few broken ones. This is a nice biscuit to have on the side — like a not-too-sweet version of melba toast — that you can stack up like dominoes as Venetians do alongside a dessert such as Crema di mascarpone (page 262) or to eat with Mostarda (page 28).

__Sprinkle the dried (*or crumble up the fresh*) yeast into a bowl, add the lukewarm milk & whisk together. Leave until the yeast starts to activate & bubble up a bit. Cream the butter & sugar with electric beaters.
__Add the activating yeast to the creamed butter & then sift in the flour, egg white & a pinch of salt. Mix well with a wooden spoon, then with your hands, adding a little extra flour to the dough & your hands, to get a nice soft ball. Make a cross on top, cover the bowl with a cloth & leave in a draught-free warm place for a couple of hours until puffed up. Line a very large baking tray (or 2 trays) with baking paper.
__Punch the dough down & divide into 4 salami about 30 cm (12 inches) long & 4 cm (1½ inches) across, using a little extra flour if necessary. Put them on your baking tray. Cover loosely with a cloth & leave for 1½–2 hours until well risen. Preheat your oven to 180°C (350°F/Gas 4).
__Bake for 15–20 minutes until light golden & cooked. Turn off the oven & leave inside to cool completely for 24 hours — they will harden in this time. Slice each salami into 2 mm thick slices with very decisive knife movements.
__Preheat your oven to 160°C (315°F/Gas 2–3). Lay the pieces of biscuit on a baking tray & bake for 10 minutes, turning once, until crisp but not brown. Cool & store in an airtight container.

Makes many many

Torta di amaretti

Amaretti tart

Pastry:

75 g (2½ oz) cold unsalted
  butter, chopped
250 g (9 oz/2 cups) cake
  (00) flour
1 teaspoon baking powder
75 g (2½ oz) sugar
2 eggs

Crema:

2 eggs
125 g (4½ oz) caster (superfine)
  sugar
100 g (3½ oz) blanched
  almonds or coarsely
  ground almonds

about 80 g (2¾ oz) amaretti
  biscuits
about 4 tablespoons rum
  or cognac
2 heaped tablespoons
  orange marmalade

*My sister-in-law, Luisa, taught me this recipe. She has been making it for a while
& doesn't remember where she got it from. It's essentially a tart made up of layers:
pastry, marmalade, amaretti biscuits &, finally, a creamy egg custard with ground
almonds. The number of amaretti you need to cover the bottom of your pastry will
depend on their size — if they're small you'll need a few more. If you have homemade
orange marmalade it's great in this tart.*

__To make the pastry, mix the butter in a bowl with the flour, baking powder
& sugar until crumbly looking. Add the eggs & mix until it comes together.
(*Alternatively, pulse together in a food processor.*) Press the dough into a ball,
flatten a bit & cover with plastic. Chill for at least an hour in the fridge (*you
can make this a day in advance, or even freeze it at this stage*).
__To make the crema, beat the eggs with the sugar for about 5 minutes
until thick & pale. If you are using blanched almonds, pulse them in a food
processor until coarsely ground. Whisk the ground almonds into the egg
mixture with a fork.
__Put the amaretti on a plate. Splash bit by bit with the alcohol until they
have absorbed most of it. Heat your oven to 170°C (325°F/Gas 3).
__Wet a sheet of baking paper (about 33 x 48 cm/13 x 19 inches), scrunching
it up completely. Then un-scrunch it & shake off the water. Flatten it onto
your work surface, drying it with a clean cloth. Roll out your dough on
the paper with another sheet of paper on top to help roll it without sticking
to the rolling pin. Roll the pastry out to line the base & side of a 24 cm
(9½ inch) springform tin. If the weather is hot, you may have to refrigerate
the pastry again. Peel away the top layer of paper & lift the pastry & base
layer of paper into your tin, pressing the pastry down well (*you will find this
easier to do using floured fingers*). The pastry rim should be about 2 cm (¾ inch)
lower than the top of the tin, & the paper underneath the pastry will help
you lift it out for serving.

__Prick the pastry base a few times with a fork. Spread the marmalade over the base of the pastry. Layer the soaked amaretti biscuits over the marmalade in a single layer, completely covering the base.

__Gently pour the crema into the tin — it should come almost to the top of the pastry. Cook the tart for 30–40 minutes until the filling is well set & a bit cracked here & there & the pastry is cooked through & pale golden. If you like, you can dust the tart with icing sugar to serve, but I think it is sweet enough as it is.

Serves 8–10

Gelato al limone

Lemon ice cream

zest of 1 lemon, cut into
  big strips
225 g (8 oz/1 cup) sugar
150 ml (5 fl oz) lemon juice
250 ml (9 fl oz/1 cup) chilled
  cream

__Put the lemon zest & sugar in a small saucepan with 125 ml (4 fl oz/ ½ cup) water. Bring to the boil, stirring to dissolve the sugar. Lower the heat & simmer gently, without stirring, for 5–10 minutes until the mixture becomes syrupy & tastes lemon zesty. Fish out the pieces of zest. Cool the mixture, then pour in the lemon juice.

__Whisk the cream until it's fairly stiff & then whisk in the cool lemon syrup. When cool, transfer to a container with a lid & put in the freezer. After an hour give the mixture an energetic whisk with a hand whisk or electric mixer. Put it back in the freezer & then whisk again after another couple of hours. When the ice cream is nearly firm, give one last whisk.

__Alternatively, pour into your ice cream machine & churn, following the manufacturer's instructions.

Serves 6

✥Sgroppino✥

Lemon chill

200 g (7 oz) lemon ice cream
  (page 267)
about 4 tablespoons
  chilled prosecco
about 2 tablespoons
  chilled vodka

You can make your own or buy lemon ice cream for this recipe. If you are making your own ice cream, make it the day before so that it has time to become firm & then all you have to do on the day is briefly whizz the ice cream with the alcohol. You can add as much prosecco & vodka as you like here depending how soft your ice cream is & how strong you want this to be. Since I like to serve this after lunch, I've made it fairly mild, bearing in mind that you may have started the meal with prosecco, then moved onto wine & are not looking at passing out for the afternoon. It's much more summery with less alcohol anyway. Many people serve this as a palate cleanser instead of as a dessert. If it's very hot then put your glasses in the freezer for a few minutes before serving.

__Scoop the ice cream into a blender. Splash in the prosecco & vodka & whizz (*the more alcohol you add the more liquidy the mixture will end up*). Pour into glasses & serve at once before it melts completely!

Serves 2

Sbriciolona

Crumbler cake

200 g (9 oz) unpeeled almonds
1 egg
140 g (5 oz/⅔ cup) sugar
1 teaspoon vanilla extract
250 g (9 oz) unsalted butter,
  softened
250 g (9 oz/2 cups) plain
  (all-purpose) flour
thick cream or ice cream,
  to serve

Be prepared to tread on crumbs around the table after eating sbriciolona. Sbriciolare is Italian for 'crumble', & that's exactly what the name implies: crumbly. This is beautiful with sweetened whipped or thick cream that the crumbs can cling to, or just with a glass of something moscato-ish. In Venice, fragolino, a red or white sweet wine, is what they like to drink.

__Preheat your oven to 180°C (350°F/Gas 4). Use a blob from the butter to grease a 28 cm (11 inch) springform cake tin & lightly dust it with flour. Put the almonds in a food processor & pulse until quite fine but with some chunks left (alternatively, bash them with your rolling pin).

__Whip the egg with the sugar & vanilla until nice & creamy. Put the softened butter on a plate & mash until smooth but not melted. Gradually whisk the flour, butter & a pinch of salt into the egg mixture. Add the ground almonds & work them in with your hands to make a rough pastry.

__Pat the mixture into your tin, dollops at a time, flattening it to roughly cover the base. It won't look perfect but will spread while baking. Bake for about 40 minutes until golden brown.

__Cool, then cut into wedges if you can (it's crumbly). To serve, either whip some cream with a little vanilla extract & sugar, or simply serve with thick cream which holds the crumbs in its cloud of thickness.

Serves 8–10

Mele cotte con amaretti

Cooked apples with amaretti

4 lovely apples
10 small amaretti biscuits
25 g (1 oz) sultanas
3 tablespoons sugar
2 tablespoons grappa or brandy
30 g (1 oz) unsalted butter
375 ml (13 fl oz/1½ cups)
  white wine
2 strips of orange peel

This is a very simple, homestyle dessert. I like to make it with 2 green & 2 red apples – not because I can see any difference at the end, but it looks great before it goes into the oven! If you're serving more than 4 people, you can easily add a couple more apples & just increase the other ingredients accordingly. It's best to use a baking dish that fits the apples fairly snugly.

__Preheat your oven to 180°C (350°F/Gas 4). Remove the apple cores with a corer, leaving the apples in one piece. Prick the peel a few times with the point of your knife.

__Using a mortar & pestle (or rolling pin or heavy bottle) crush the amaretti with the sultanas & 1 tablespoon of the sugar until roughly smashed. Add the grappa or brandy, mix well & stuff into the centre of each apple.

__Put the apples in a baking dish & sprinkle a tablespoon of sugar evenly over the tops. Divide the butter into four & put a blob on top of each apple. Pour the wine around the apples, then add the final tablespoon of sugar & the orange peel to the wine. Cover loosely with foil & bake for about 20 minutes until tender. Uncover & cook for another 20 minutes, basting the apples with the pan juices a couple of times, until they are well cooked, but not split.

__Remove the cooked apples from the dish, turn the oven right up & put the dish back in to reduce the sauce until golden (or do this on the stovetop). Serve the apples warm or at room temperature with the juice spooned over & around.

Serves 4

❧Gelato di amaretto❧

Amaretto ice cream

70 g (2½ oz) amaretti biscuits
250 ml (9 fl oz/1 cup) milk
3 egg yolks
100 g (3½ oz) sugar
½ teaspoon vanilla extract
250 ml (9 fl oz/1 cup) cream

This is not as amaro as you may think. It has a gentle Italian elegance about it, I find, & goes well after any meal, but especially autumn & winter dishes like Bigoli in salsa or duck.

__Crush the amaretti very well with a mortar & pestle or rolling pin. Put the milk in a heavy-based small-ish pan & heat gently; meanwhile, whip the yolks very well with the sugar & vanilla until pale & thick. Before the milk comes to the boil, whisk a little into your creamy eggs, whipping so that the eggs don't scramble. When it's well mixed tip it all back into the pan over very low heat & whisk well for a couple of minutes — just to slightly cook the eggs but please don't scramble them into lumps.

__Remove from the heat & cool a dash. Whisk in the cold cream & then the amaretti biscuits. Leave to cool completely then transfer to a container with a lid & put in the freezer. After an hour give the mixture an energetic whisk with a hand whisk or electric mixer. Put it back in the freezer & then whisk again after another couple of hours. When the ice cream is nearly firm, give one last whisk & put it back in the freezer to firm overnight.

__Alternatively, pour into your ice-cream machine & churn, following the manufacturer's instructions, then leave overnight in the freezer to firm up.

Serves 4–6

Zabaione

Eggs & marsala

4 egg yolks
80 g (2¾ oz) caster (superfine)
   sugar
100 ml (3½ fl oz) marsala

Here zabaione is served the classic way, sweet & warm. But you may like to add some whipped cream to make it a softer pudding… If so, whip 185 ml (6 fl oz/ ¾ cup) cream until lovely & billowy, then fold it gently but thoroughly into the zabaione. You could also add a pinch of ground cinnamon or grated lemon zest or a dash of vanilla extract although I love the simplicity of marsala here. Another variation is to replace the marsala with the same amount of espresso — use your empty egg shells to measure the marsala… 6 half shells will give you the right amount. In Italy, zabaione was traditionally served to the newlywed man so he had energy to get through the wedding night!

__Quarter-fill a pan with water. Put the pan on the heat & bring the water to the boil, then reduce to a low simmer.

__Put the egg yolks, sugar & a few drops of the marsala in a wide stainless steel bowl & beat with electric beaters until thick & creamy. Lift the bowl onto the pot of simmering water, making sure the bowl doesn't touch the water. Turn the heat to the lowest possible level. Beat the mixture over the hot water for about 20 minutes until it is *voluminoso*, adding the rest of the marsala bit by bit; when the mixture is very thick & creamy add the rest. Now & then gently scrape down the side of the bowl, trying your best not to let any cooked bits get into the pudding. After about 20 minutes of beating, the mixture should be thick & creamy, so remove it from the heat & keep whisking a bit while it cools.

__Spoon into lovely glass cups & serve while still slightly warm. Or keep covered in the fridge. Serve with baicoli (page 265), amaretti or other hard biscuits that you can use as a spoon.

Serves 4–6

❦ *Gelato di zabaione* ❦

Zabaione ice cream

6 egg yolks
220 g (7¾ oz/1 cup) sugar
375 ml (13 fl oz/1½ cups) milk
125 ml (4 fl oz/½ cup) marsala
375 ml (13 fl oz/1½ cups)
   cream

I love this gelato. Serve on its own or with a plain biscuit like a baicolo (page 265). I hope you have a big ice-cream machine for this, but if not, just make half a portion. Use your empty egg shells to measure the marsala… about 5 half shells full here.

__Whip the egg yolks & sugar until pale & thick. While you are beating, slowly heat the milk in a heavy-based pan (*not too large*). Before the milk comes to the boil, whisk a little of it into the creamy eggs, whipping so that the eggs don't scramble. When it is all mixed together, scrape the whole lot back into the pan & return to very low heat, whisking well for a couple of minutes, not to thicken the sauce but to slightly cook the eggs — but don't let the eggs scramble into any lumps.

__Remove the pot from the heat & allow to cool. Whisk in the marsala & stir in the cold cream, then leave to cool completely. Transfer to a container with a lid & put in the freezer. After an hour give the mixture an energetic whisk with a hand whisk or electric mixer. Put it back in the freezer & then whisk again after another couple of hours. When the ice cream is nearly firm, give one last whisk and put back in the freezer to firm overnight.

__Alternatively, pour into an ice-cream machine & churn, following the manufacturer's instructions. Scoop into an airtight container & freeze.

Serves 6–8

Bussola

'S' or round biscuits

125 g (4½ oz) cold unsalted
  butter, chopped
250 g (9 oz/2 cups) cake
  (00) flour
110 g (3¾ oz) sugar
2 egg yolks
1½ teaspoons vanilla extract
1½ teaspoons finely grated
  lemon zest
2 tablespoons milk

These are the famous s-shaped or plain round firm biscuits that are great to serve with something like fragolino & come in many variations. They are also great with a small dish of wild strawberries & another of vanilla ice cream. These must be the ones that the boatman said come from Burano, with its lovely coloured houses… they are kept in underwear drawers because of their beautiful smell & last forever because of the citrus. Only in Venice could I believe such a tale.

__Mix the butter with the flour & sugar until crumbly looking (*rather like damp sand*). Combine the egg yolks, vanilla extract, lemon zest & milk in a bowl. Pour into the bowl & mix until it comes together. (Alternatively, pulse together in a food processor.) Turn out onto a board & bring it together to make a fat 20 cm (8 inch) long log. Wrap in plastic wrap & put in the fridge for about an hour or more.
__Preheat your oven to 170°C (325°F/Gas 3). Line two baking trays with baking paper. You will need a lightly floured surface & flour for your hands.
__Keep half the dough in the fridge to keep it cool while you work with the other half. Cut slices about 5 mm (¼ inch) thick along the log & roll each slice out to 8 cm (3 inches) x 1 cm (½ inch) thick. Form each one into an s-shape. (*Alternatively, roll them into 10 cm/4 inch ropes & join the ends to make circles instead.*)
__Put each 'S' or circle on the baking tray. Bake for 10–15 minutes or so until pale but golden here & there — they shouldn't be too hard as they will harden once out of the oven.

Makes about 50

Focaccia Veneziana

Venetian focaccia

20 g (¾ oz) fresh yeast or
  3 teaspoons dried
250 ml (9 fl oz/1 cup) warm
  milk
125 g (4½ oz) sugar
100 g (3½ oz) unsalted butter,
  melted & cooled
3 egg yolks
400 g (14 oz) cake (00) flour
a pinch of salt
finely grated zest of
  1 small lemon

Topping:
80 g (2¾ oz) sugar
2 good tablespoons
  large-granule sugar

This has little in common with the bread called focaccia, but is more a brioche-pandoro thing. I tasted one from the pasticceria Puppa in Cannareggio & was completely sold on it, so I found a recipe in my sister-in-law's old book 'A Tola co I Nostri Veci' by Mariu Salvatori de Zuliani (thank goodness, I had Luisa to translate the Venetian dialect instructions to me).

__Dissolve the yeast in the milk & whip with a whisk. Add the sugar, butter, egg yolks, flour & salt, mixing at the end with your hands or a strong whisk, to form a soft pap. Cover with plastic wrap, then a cloth & leave for 12 hours in warm-ish place until well risen. Uncover & mix it all again with your hands (*even though it is very soft*), kneading in the lemon zest. Lightly butter a 2.25 litre (9 cup) tin (*or use a paper mould*).
__Plop the dough into the tin as evenly as possible — it will seem as if there is a lot of room left, but it will rise, so cover the top again with plastic wrap & then a tea towel & leave in a warm place again for a couple of hours. Preheat your oven to 180°C (350°F/Gas 4).
__Remove the plastic wrap & bake the dough for about 40 minutes until golden on top, covering with foil for the last 15 minutes if you think it is browning too much. A skewer poked into the centre should come out clean.
__Meanwhile make the sugar syrup. Put the sugar in a small pan with 3 tablespoons water, stir to dissolve the sugar, then let it simmer without stirring for 5–8 minutes until thickened a bit. Cool for a moment & then brush over the cooled focaccia. Sprinkle the sugar granules over the top so they stick.

Makes 1 big cake…

$\backsim$ I N D E X $\multimap$

INDEX

INDEX

INDEX

GRAZIE

__To all who helped in the making of this book —
I am truly grateful.

__Thank you Artemis and Kyriakos for showing
me the good life in Venice. Thank you Luisa (for
being my half-Venetian sister in law!) and for
making the collecting and cooking so much smoother
and grazioso. Thank you to your sister, Lidia, your
nephew, Andrea, and your mom, Dina.

__I had the fortuna of meeting amazing Venetians
who made my journeys wonderful. Thank you
all for your spontaneous help: Sergia Regolino,
Alimentari in Calle dei do Mori; Marinella Jop
from 'La Buona Forchetta' ristorante; Giorgia
from Rialto fish market (Pescheria Giorgia and
Gianni Fabbris); Alvise Ceccato from ristorante
'Antica Adelaide'; Licio Sfriso from 'trattoria
alla Madonna'; Stefano Nicolao from Nicolao
Atelier costume hire for allowing us into your
beautiful costume kingdom; Valerio Pagnacco and
Mariagrazia Dammico, Flavia Cordioli Mognetti
for your gracious help; Houshang Rachtian from
Casa d'Aste Antiques for gallantly allowing us to
photograph your red monkey; to the artist Gianni
Roberti for your painting on the wall of the
Antica Mola trattoria. Thank you also to Franco,
Sebastian, and Stefano.

__To all away from Venice — thank you Mario,
Wilma, Angela-Maria, Lisa, Richard, Sue,
Andrea, Barbara, Mariella, Claudia, Marzia,
Scilla and Roberto, Luciano and Stefania,
Antonella, Paolo, Julia, Jem, Anabelle, Peta, Anna,
Jan, Rebecca, Nicci and Marisa for all your very
much appreciated help and encouragement.

__Thank you Anna Rosa Migone from Saena Vetus
Antiques in Siena for allowing us to use some of
your valued pieces.

__Thank you Popsi for your solidity and for
adapting so well to all situations, and to my
beautiful wonders, Yasmine and Cassia — thank you
for making everything so much more fun always.

__Thank you Mom, Dad, Ludi and Nin for your
support always.

__Thank you to all at Murdoch Books, to Jane and
Jo and the many involved in production. Thanks
Michelle, for going further than you had to. Thank
you Kay for dealing the card of opportunity.

__To my team. A grande thank you: Michail, I
acknowledge your ability to style mountains out of
molehills. Manos, your beautiful sensitivity with
your camera, and Lisa — the best art director friend
one could hope for.

Tess x

INSPIRATION COOKBOOKS:

La cucina del Veneto, Emilia Valli
A tola co i nostri veci, Mariù Salvatori de Zuliani
A Tavola con I Dogi, Pino Agostini, Alvise Zorzi
Venice and Food, Sally Spector

INSPIRATION READING:

The Passion, Jeanette Winterson
Across the River and into the Trees, Ernest Hemingway
The City of Falling Angels, John Berendt
Acqua Alta, Donna Leon
Venetian Stories, Jane Turner Rylands
Venice for Pleasure, J.G. Links
The Stones of Venice, John Ruskin